TROUT
ALMANAC

Colorado & Wyoming

Kim Long

Johnson Books: Boulder

First Edition
1 2 3 4 5 6 7 8 9

ISBN 1-55566-014-2
LCCCN 87-81305

Printed in the United States of America by
    Johnson Publishing Company
    1880 South 57th Court
    Boulder, Colorado 80301

This book is dedicated to my grandfather, who never fished for trout, but knew what it meant.

Thanks! Material in this book was collected from many sources, including . . .

Colorado Department of Health: *Dennis Anderson*
Colorado Division of Wildlife: *Dave Weber, Steve Cassin, Lou Kroeckel, Jim Satterfield, Phil Goebel, Rita Green*
Colorado State Climatology Office (Fort Collins)
Colorado State Engineer's Office (Division of Water Resources): *John Kaliszewski, Charles Shaffer*
Denver Museum of Natural History: *Larry Sessions*
Denver Public Library (Government Publications)
Ed Pearl, Meterologist
Interfluve (Bozeman, Montana): *Dale Miller*
Johnson Books (Boulder, Colorado): *Barbara Mussil, Michael McNierney, Richard Croog, Janice Brown*
National Climatic Data Center (Asheville, North Carolina)
National Park Service: *Jim Olsen*
Pattern Research   (Denver, Colorado): *Leif Smith, Pat Wagner*
Oakland Museum (Aquatic Resources Department): *Christopher Richard*
Hugh Gardner
U.S. Fish and Wildlife Service: *Bruce Rosenlund*
U.S.G.S. (Colorado Water Resources Division): *Harold Petsch, Barbara Condron*
U.S.G.S. (Wyoming Water Resources Division): *David A. Peterson, Sherry Green*
Wind River Indian Reservation: *Edith Johnson*
Wyoming Game and Fish Department: *Mike Stone, Bud Stewart*

Table of Contents ▬▬▬

How to Use This Book *1*

Trout Facts *2*

Trout Spawning Seasons *4*

Water Temperature Range *4*

Trout Food Sources *5*

Trout Parts *5*

The Rocky Mountain Trout Diet *6*

Caddisflies *7*

Midges *8*

Stoneflies *8*

Craneflies *10*

Mayflies *11*

Other Aquatic Insects *14*

Terrestrials and Non-Insect Foods *15*

Fly Rods *16*

Fly Line Symbols *16*

Fly Line Weights *17*

Leaders *17*

Trout Flies *18*

Insect Hatches *22*

Catch and Release *33*

The Color of Trout *33*

Measuring Trout *34*

Rocky Mountain Danger *34*

Premium Trout Fishing *36*

Map of Wyoming Streams *40*

Map of Colorado Streams *41*

Trout Streams *42*

Colorado Trout Streams *44*

Wyoming Trout Streams *74*

Weather Conditions *102*
Rocky Mountain Weather Rules of Thumb *102*
Lightning *103*
Flash Floods *104*
Hypothermia *104*
Wind Chill *105*
Colorado Weather *106*
Wyoming Weather *114*
Streamflow Standard Deviation Values *120*
Fly Fishing Schools *125*
Books *126*
Fly Fishing Stores *127*
Organizations *128*
Wyoming Mileage Chart *129*
Colorado Mileage Chart *130*
Colorado Fishing Information *131*
Colorado Fishing Regulations *132*
Map of Colorado Fishing Zones *133*
Rocky Mountain National Park Regulations ... *139*
Wyoming Fishing Regulations *140*
Map of Wyoming Fishing Zones *141*
Grand Teton National Park Regulatons *145*
Map of Yellowstone Fishing Zones *146*
Yellowstone Fishing Regulations *147*
Wind River Reservation Regulations *149*
Index *150*
Fishing Knots .... *inside front and back covers*

color illustrations appear facing page 74

How to Use This Book ____

Fishing for trout in the Rocky Mountains can be an exercise in futility or a major thrill. For many people there is no in-between, because the elusive trout requires more information, experience, and ability than is available to the average fisherman. The basic concept of *The Trout Almanac* is that accessible information will make any trout fishing experience more rewarding. However, there are no magic formulas, tactics, or tricks—this book and other useful publications can only provide a little help along the way.

The Trout Almanac is organized to help develop a planned approach to Rocky Mountain fishing adventures . . .

- **Picking a time**. Seasonal information about fishing conditions is provided in three areas: **a)** weather conditions, both historical averages for the two states and regional climatic conditions; **b)** water conditions that affect trout activity listed in monthly streamflow values and water temperatures; **c)** insect activity that indicates when specific insects are hatching.

- **Choosing equipment**. General guidelines for fly fishing gear specify the range of sizes available for poles and lines, as well as recommended combinations, and the most popular regional trout flies.

- **Being prepared**. Use this book to understand the potentially dangerous conditions that a fisherman can encounter in the Rocky Mountains and the specific regulations that apply to certain fishing areas.

With all this preparation, it is still up to the individual to make the trout fishing experience a success. Good luck!

Trout Facts ════════════

Brown Trout   Salmo *trutta*

- Range. Originally from Europe and first introduced to the U.S. in 1883. Established populations are now found in more than forty states, including all western states.
- Body. Length is 4 1/2 —5 times depth; dorsal fin has 10-13 rays; anal fin has 9-10 rays; tail is almost square in mature fish; vomerine teeth have a double zigzag row on the vomer.
- Coloring. Golden-brown to olive coloring with large brown and black spots on back and sides, including dorsal fin; spots may have "halos" of a lighter brown color; some red and, or orange spots on lateral body surfaces; dorsal and adipose fins sometimes have orange or red fringe and, or spots; lower sides and belly have yellow or white tinge.

Cutthroat Trout   Salmo *clarki*

- Range. Native to the western U.S.
- Body. Length is 4-5 times depth; dorsal fin has 11 rays; anal fin has 8-12 rays; tail is slightly forked.
- Coloring. Distinctive orange or red markings on and below the lower jaw; body coloration varies among the subspecies from light-green to silver or gold; darker spots on lateral and posterior body, dorsal fin, and tail; a pink or reddish band along the sides may be visible; males display red bellys during breeding season.
- Subspecies. Colorado cutthroat (Salmo *clarkii pleuriticus*); Greenback trout (Salmo *clarkii stomias*); Lahontan cutthroat (Salmo *clarkii henshawi*); Rio Grande cutthroat (Salmo *clarkii virginalis*); Utah cutthroat (Salmo *clarkii utah*); Yellowstone cutthroat (Salmo *clarkii lewisi*); Snake River cutthroat (Salmo *clarki*).

Golden Trout   Salmo *aguabonita*

- Range. Native to California, now found east to Wyoming.
- Body. Length about 5 times depth; tail is slightly forked; dorsal and anal fins have 11 rays.
- Coloring. Body is mostly green or olive; bright reddish lateral

stripe with yellow or golden tint on lower sides with some red on lower sides and belly; dorsal fin has orange marking; anal and ventral fins have white tips; parr marks are sometimes present (about 10); darker spots on head and upper body to the lateral line, caudal peduncle, caudal, adipose, and dorsal fins.

Rainbow Trout   Salmo *gairdneri*

- Range. Native to the west coast of North America, from Mexico to Aleutian Islands of Alaska, now established across the continent.
- Body. Length about 4 1/2 times depth; anal fin has a maximum of 12 rays; dorsal fin has 11 rays; tail is forked; no hyoid teeth (on the back of the tongue).
- Coloring. Green or blue-green back with silver sides and lighter belly coloring; black or dark spots are heavy in stream-dwelling fish on head, body and fins; spots light or absent in lake fish; red or pink lateral band on sides.

Brook Trout   Salvelinus *fontinalus*

- Range. Native to northeastern North America, now found throughout the U.S.
- Body. Length about 5 times depth; dorsal fin has 10 rays; anal fin has 9 rays; tail almost square with almost no fork.
- Coloring. Body is dark green on back, blue to blue-green on sides, white to red on belly; red spots with blue "halos" on sides; yellow or pale spots on sides; dark irregular "worm" markings on back and dorsal fin; lower fins have pink coloring edged with white on the leading edge; teeth on head of the vomer; males develop orange coloring on belly during spawning.

Lake Trout (Mackinaw)   Salvelinus *namaycush*

- Range. Native to Canada and the Great Lakes, now widespread in cold-water lakes.
- Body. Length about 4 times depth; dorsal fin has 11 rays; anal fin has 11 rays; tail distinctly forked; raised tooth crest on the head of the vomer.
- Coloring. Body is grey-green, blue-gray to green; pale spots on sides and back; spots on dorsal, adipose, and caudal fins; paired fins may have some orange coloring.

Spawning Seasons⸺

JAN•FEB•MAR•APR•MAY•JUN•JUL•AUG•SEP•OCT•NOV•DEC

Brook
Brown
Cutthroat
Golden
Lake
Rainbow

Temperature Range⸺

These temperature ranges mark the optimum conditions for feeding.

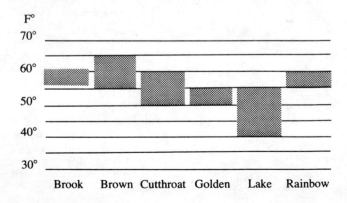

Food Sources

Brook   *larva, nymphs, adult aquatic insects, worms, crustaceans,*
    terrestrials
Brown   *larva, nymphs, adult aquatic insects, worms, crayfish,*
    terrestrials, mollusks, immature and smaller fish
Cutthroat   *larvae, nymphs, adult aquatic insects (especially cad-*
    disflies), beetles, crustaceans, grasshoppers and
    leafhoppers, other terrestrials
Golden   *larva, nymphs, adult aquatic insects (especially cad-*
    disflies), crustaceans, terrestrials
Lake   *large crustaceans, invertebrates, kokanee, whitefish, scul-*
    pin, ciscoes, and other lake-dwelling fish
Rainbow   *larva, nymphs, adult aquatic insects, worms, crusta-*
    ceans, terrestrials, immature and smaller fish

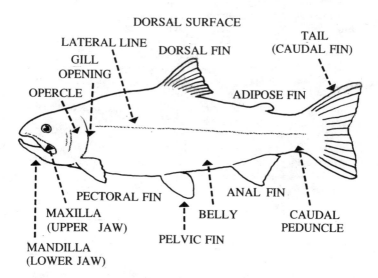

DORSAL SURFACE

LATERAL LINE   DORSAL FIN   TAIL
    (CAUDAL FIN)
GILL
OPENING

OPERCLE   ADIPOSE FIN

PECTORAL FIN   ANAL FIN

MAXILLA   BELLY   CAUDAL
(UPPER   JAW)   PEDUNCLE

MANDILLA   PELVIC FIN
(LOWER JAW)

The Rocky Mountain Trout Diet

The trout diet is composed of insects, crustaceans, and smaller fish. Insects—both aquatic and terrestrial—are the major source of food for trout. Because of the climate in the Rocky Mountains, only aquatic insects are available year-round as a food source. During the summer months when air temperatures are warm enough, hatching and mating activities of aquatic insects can be intense, and trigger wild feeding frenzies in the region's streams and rivers.

In general, the timing of an insect hatch is determined by specific characteristics of the species. However, insects within the same species that develop in different geographic locations or altitudes may hatch on different schedules. Hatch schedules are also affected by variables such as temperature, availability of food, and photoperiods (the length and amount of available light during the insect life cycle). Artificial changes in temperature for aquatic insects can occur because of reservoirs and power plants, producing earlier hatches than elsewhere in a river system. Artificial changes in the insects' food sources can also occur from pollution, floods, and weather extremes, producing delayed or reduced hatches. Artificial changes in photoperiods can occur from excess sediments in the water (from erosion, construction, and flooding) which reduce the available light and also delay the hatching schedule.

The hatching charts in this book show the range of time that hatching usually occurs in Colorado and Wyoming. In general, the beginning dates are more applicable to lower altitudes, and the middle-to-end periods more common at higher altitudes. Predicting more accurate hatching times is not possible given the wide variation in altitude and weather in the Rocky Mountains, but local fly fishing shops are usually aware of the conditions in their area.

Hatching Chart begins on page 22.

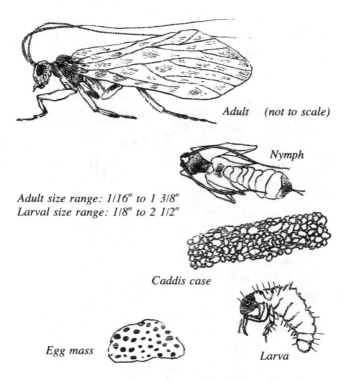

Adult   (not to scale)

Nymph

Adult size range: 1/16" to 1 3/8"
Larval size range: 1/8" to 2 1/2"

Caddis case

Egg mass

Larva

■ **Caddisflies** (also known as grannoms or sedges). The larvae and pupae stages of caddisflies live under the water. Most caddisflies construct cases during this period, made of leaves, small sticks, and organic debris from the streambed. Trout often eat these cases. Caddisflies are identifiable at this stage because each species has its own distinctive case-building method. Caddisfly larvae develop into pupae, which float to the surface of the water. The pupal skin is discarded on the surface and the adult flies away to rest and mate. Caddisflies lay their eggs in the water, becoming a food source for trout in the process. Adult caddisflies are primarily active at night.

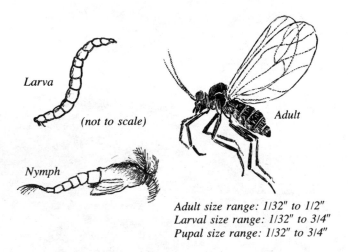

Larva

(not to scale)

Nymph

Adult

Adult size range: 1/32" to 1/2"
Larval size range: 1/32" to 3/4"
Pupal size range: 1/32" to 3/4"

- **Midges**. Eggs are laid under the water, and the larval and pupal stages remain under the surface (larvae are sometimes called bloodworms). Adults emerge from the pupal stage just under the water's surface, and trout feed on them often during this part of the cycle.

- **Stoneflies** (also known as willow flies; the Giant Stonefly is called a salmonfly). Stonefly nymphs live under the water, and are often the target of feeding trout. Nymphs crawl out out of the water before the adults emerge. Stoneflies emerge throughout summer and fall months. As a rule, adults in summer are active after dark, and those in fall are active during the day. Trout feed on adult stoneflies when they drop onto the water's surface during mating or when laying eggs.

Adult

(not to scale)

Adult size range: 1/4" to 2"
Nymph size range: 1/4" to 2"

Instars are growth stages of nymphs

Eggs

Instar

Instar

Instar

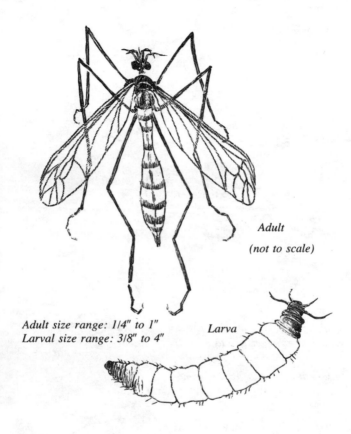

Adult

(not to scale)

Adult size range: 1/4" to 1"
Larval size range: 3/8" to 4"   *Larva*

■ **Craneflies**. Cranefly larvae are often very large and can be an important form of food for trout. Pupation occurs under the water in some species, in mud or damp streamside conditions in other species. Adults emerge throughout the summer and early fall. Adult craneflies are most active at sunset and early evening and are often called spinners (not to be confused with adult mayflies).

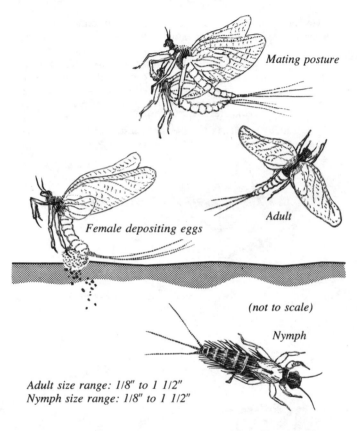

Mating posture

Adult

Female depositing eggs

(not to scale)

Nymph

Adult size range: 1/8" to 1 1/2"
Nymph size range: 1/8" to 1 1/2"

■ **Mayflies** (also known as duns or drakes). Mayfly nymphs often hatch in synchronous or near-synchronous schedules (mayfly nymphs are larvae; mayflies do not have a pupal stage). Nymphs of the same species have relatively short hatching periods, from a few hours to a few weeks, but several generations will often emerge in the same season. Trout feed mostly on mayflies when the adult insects are emerging from the nymph forms. Emerging adults are often called duns (or subimagos) and the emerging style varies according to species: some nymphs crawl out of the water before shedding their skins, others shed their skin on the bottom or surface of the water. The mayfly duns will shed once more before becoming fully mature (adults are referred to as spinners or imagos). The final moult occurs within 1 to 2 days, but can occur in a few hours in some genera. Adult mayflies have no digestive functions; they exist only to mate. Mating occurs during flight, often over water. After mating and egg laying, adults usually fall to the water's surface (referred to as a "spinner fall")

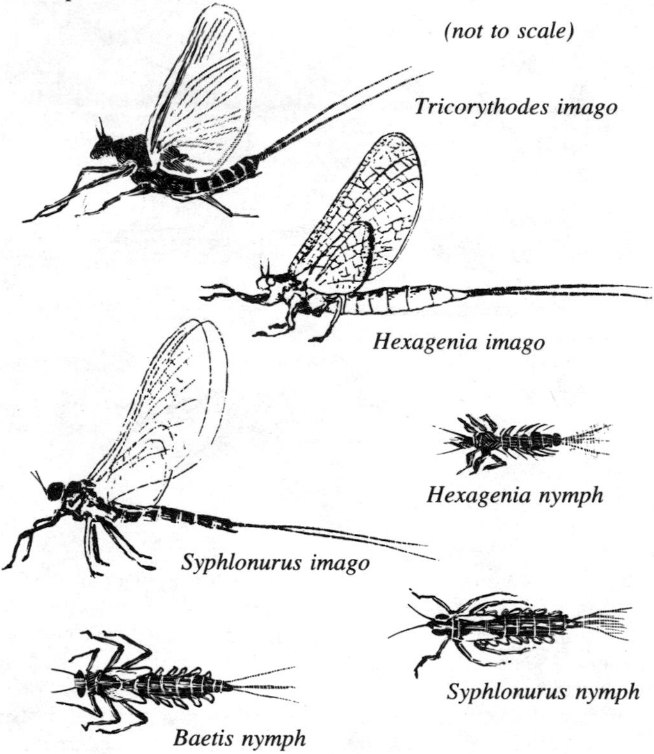

(not to scale)

Tricorythodes imago

Hexagenia imago

Hexagenia nymph

Syphlonurus imago

Syphlonurus nymph

Baetis nymph

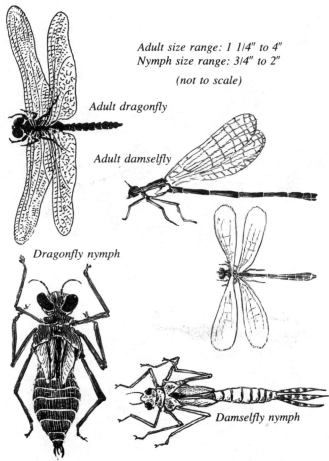

Adult size range: 1 1/4" to 4"
Nymph size range: 3/4" to 2"

(not to scale)

Adult dragonfly

Adult damselfly

Dragonfly nymph

Damselfly nymph

■ **Dragonflies and damselflies**. The large size of dragonfly and damselfly nymphs make them an attractive target for trout. Dragonfly nymphs have lengthy periods of development and are available to trout year-round. Damselfly nymphs are mostly found in the spring and early summer months.

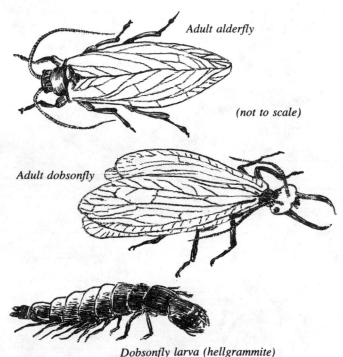

Adult alderfly

(not to scale)

Adult dobsonfly

Dobsonfly larva (hellgrammite)

Dobsonfly adult size range: 1 5/8" to 2 3/4"
Dobsonfly larval size range: 1 1/4" to 3 1/2"
Alderfly adult size range: 3/8" to 5/8"
Alderfly larval size range: 1/2" to 1"

■ **Other aquatic insects**. Additional insects that provide a food source for trout in the west include several varieties of alderflies, dobsonflies, black flies, deer flies, mosquitoes, and no-see-ums.

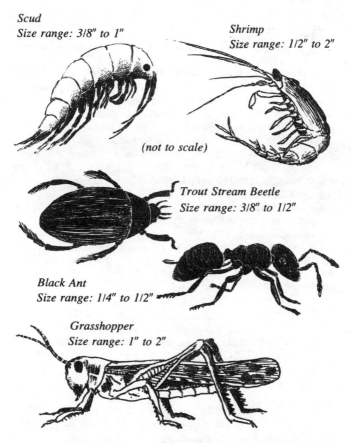

Scud
Size range: 3/8" to 1"

Shrimp
Size range: 1/2" to 2"

(not to scale)

Trout Stream Beetle
Size range: 3/8" to 1/2"

Black Ant
Size range: 1/4" to 1/2"

Grasshopper
Size range: 1" to 2"

■ **Other trout food sources**. Trout at times feed heavily on terrestrial insects which fall or are blown into the water. The most common of these in the Rockies are grasshoppers, leafhoppers, red and black ants, and flying ants. Aquatic beetles (especially the trout stream beetles) are an important food source in some areas. Also in certain areas, crustaceans (mostly freshwater shrimp, scud, and copepods) form the primary source of food at some times of the year.

Fly Rods ━━━━━━━

There is no simple formula in choosing the best fly rod size, either length or weight. Rods were once made of cane or bamboo, and the limitations of the material in turn limited the type of fly line best suited for the rod. Fly rods are now made from fiberglass, graphite, boron, or combinations of these, as well as bamboo. The characteristics of the rod material can produce rods of the same length but able to handle very different lines. Rods 7 1/2' long, for example, can be made to handle fly line weights from #2 to #6. A manufacturers recommendation or personal experimentation is a good idea.

For Rocky Mountain waters, an average rod length of 7-8' is adequate for most trout fishing situations, from the smallest streams to the major rivers. Line weights most commonly used in this region are #4-#8, with #6 or #7 a useful average. The same rod that can handle the lighter #4 line is unlikely to manage well with the heavier #8 line, however, and in the Rockies, both may be needed.

LENGTH	USE
7 feet	Streams, low water
7 1/2-8 feet	Rivers, low water
8 1/2-9 feet	Rivers, medium-to-fast water, high wind.

Fly Line Symbols ━━━━━

(based on AFTMA standards)

L	Level
DT	Double Taper
ST	Single Taper
WF	Weight Forward
F	Floating
S	Sinking
I	Intermediate (floats or sinks, depending on line dressing)
F/S	Sinking Tip

Fly Line Weights ───

NOTE: Measurement is based on the first 30 feet of the line only, not including tapered tips or leaders. 437.5 grains is equal to one ounce.

#1	60 grains
#2	80
#3	100 ── Clear, low water, sensitive fish
#4	120
#5	140 ── Average Rocky Mountain usage
#6	160
#7	185 ── Fast water, high wind
#8	210
#9	240
#10	280
#11	330
#12	380
#13	440
#14	500

LINE SIZE	FLY SIZE
#3, #4	#14-#28
#5, #6	#8-#22
#7, #8	#4-#16

Leaders ───

SIZE	FLY SIZE
0X (.011″)	#1/0—#2
1X (.010″)	#4—#6
2X (.009″)	#6—#10
3X (.008″)	#8—#12
4X (.007″)	#10—#14
5X (.006″)	#14—#18
6X (.005″)	#16—#20
7X (.004″)	#18—#24
8X (.003″)	#22—#28

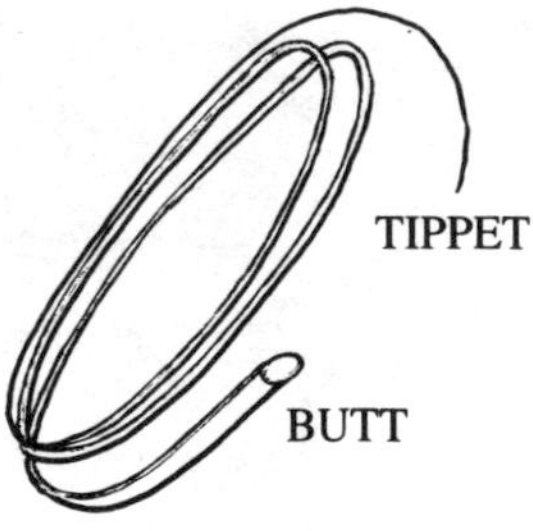

TIPPET

BUTT

Standard ready-made leader lengths

    7 1/2 feet (small streams, limited casting range)
    9 feet (average use, lakes and rivers)
    12 feet (clear water, small flies)

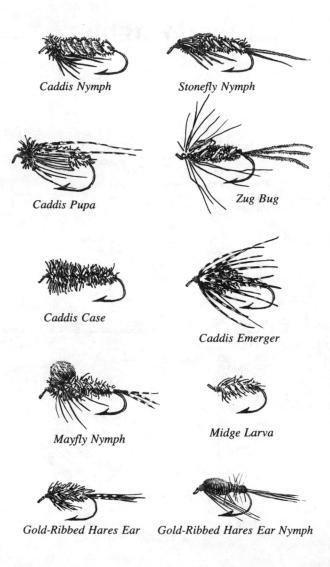

Caddis Nymph

Stonefly Nymph

Caddis Pupa

Zug Bug

Caddis Case

Caddis Emerger

Mayfly Nymph

Midge Larva

Gold-Ribbed Hares Ear

Gold-Ribbed Hares Ear Nymph

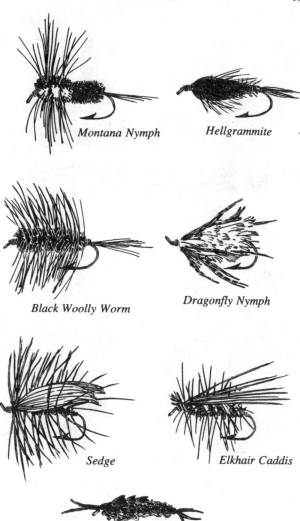

Montana Nymph

Hellgrammite

Black Woolly Worm

Dragonfly Nymph

Sedge

Elkhair Caddis

Black Stonefly

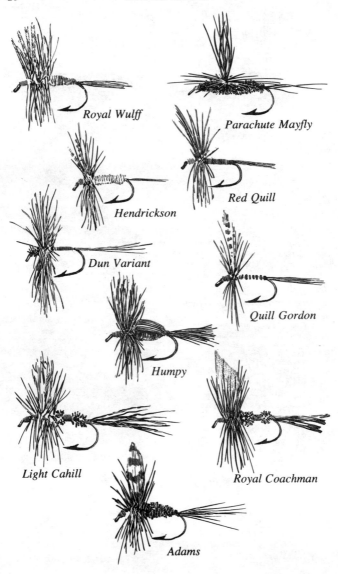

Royal Wulff

Parachute Mayfly

Hendrickson

Red Quill

Dun Variant

Quill Gordon

Humpy

Light Cahill

Royal Coachman

Adams

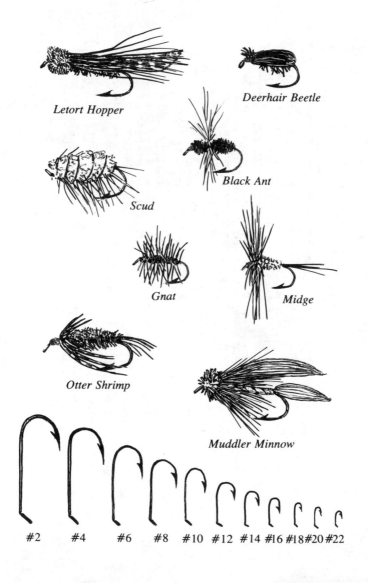

Letort Hopper

Deerhair Beetle

Scud

Black Ant

Gnat

Midge

Otter Shrimp

Muddler Minnow

#2   #4   #6   #8   #10 #12 #14 #16 #18 #20 #22

MAYFLIES

	J	F	M	A	M	J	J	A	S	O	N	D

Ametropus albarda
Watery Dun #18

Baetis sp.
Baetis Nymph #16; Bl. Quill, #16-#22; Iron Bl. Dun, #16-#22; Bl. Quill Spinner #16, #18

Baetis parvus
Baetis Nymph #16; Little Western Iron Blue Quill #18-#22

Baetis tricaudatus
Baetis Nymph #16; Dark Bl. Quill #6-22; Iron Bl. Dun #16-#22; Ginger Quill Spinner #16

Callibaetis americanus
Callibaetis Nymph #16; Grey Quill #16; Grey Quill Spinner #14, #16

Callibaetis coloradensis
Callibaetis Nymph #16; Specklewinged Dun #16; Specklewinged Spinner #14, #16

Callibaetis nigritus
Callibaetis Nymph #16; Grey Quill #16; Speckled Spinner #14, #16

Callibaetis pallidus
Callibaetis Nymph #14, #16; Pale Olive Quill #14, #16; Ginger Quill Spinner #14, #16

Centroptilum convexum
Pale Graywinged Sulphur #16, #18

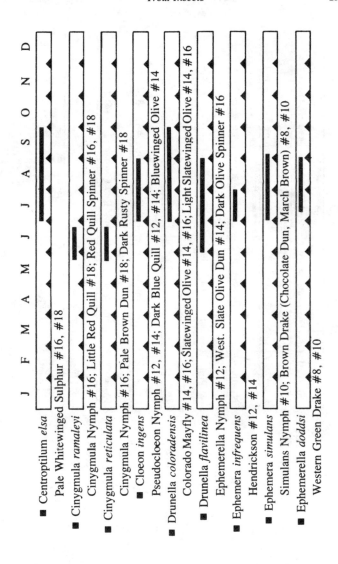

J F M A M J J A S O N D

■ Centroptilum *elsa*
Pale Whitewinged Sulphur #16, #18

■ Cinygmula *ramaleyi*
Cinygmula Nymph #16; Little Red Quill #18; Red Quill Spinner #16, #18

■ Cinygmula *reticulata*
Cinygmula Nymph #16; Pale Brown Dun #18; Dark Rusty Spinner #18

■ Cloeon *ingens*
Pseudocloeon Nymph #12, #14; Dark Blue Quill #12, #14; Bluewinged Olive #14

■ Drunella *coloradensis*
Colorado Mayfly #14, #16; Slatewinged Olive #14, #16; Light Slatewinged Olive #14, #16

■ Drunella *flavilinea*
Ephemerella Nymph #12; West. Slate Olive Dun #14; Dark Olive Spinner #16

■ Ephemera *infrequens*
Hendrickson #12, #14

■ Ephemera *simulans*
Simulans Nymph #10; Brown Drake (Chocolate Dun, March Brown) #8, #10

■ Ephemerella *doddsi*
Western Green Drake #8, #10

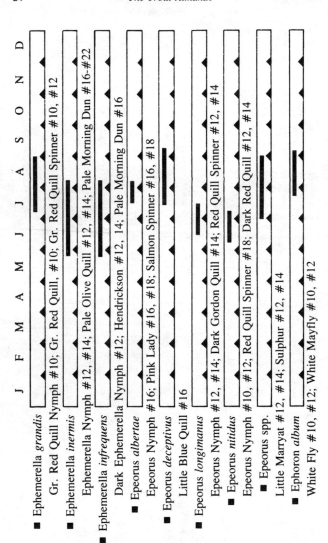

J F M A M J J A S O N D

Ephemerella *grandis*
Gr. Red Quill Nymph #10; Gr. Red Quill, #10; Gr. Red Quill Spinner #10, #12

Ephemerella *inermis*
Ephemerella Nymph #12, #14; Pale Olive Quill #12, #14; Pale Morning Dun #16-#22

Ephemerella *infrequens*
Dark Ephemerella Nymph #12; Hendrickson #12, 14; Pale Morning Dun #16

Epeorus *albertae*
Epeorus Nymph #16; Pink Lady #16, #18; Salmon Spinner #16, #18

Epeorus *deceptivus*
Little Blue Quill #16

Epeorus *longimanus*
Epeorus Nymph #12, #14; Dark Gordon Quill #14; Red Quill Spinner #12, #14

Epeorus *nitidus*
Epeorus Nymph #10, #12; Red Quill Spinner #18; Dark Red Quill #12, #14

Epeorus spp.
Little Marryat #12, #14; Sulphur #12, #14

Ephoron *album*
White Fly #10, #12; White Mayfly #10, #12

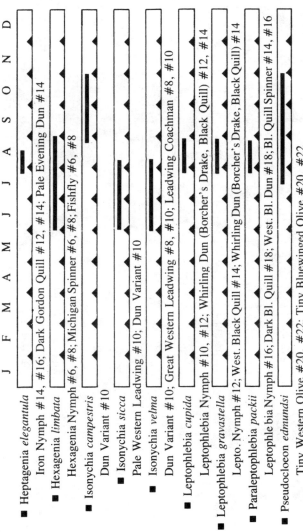

J F M A M J J A S O N D

Heptagenia elegantula
Iron Nymph #14, #16; Dark Gordon Quill #12, #14; Pale Evening Dun #14

Hexagenia limbata
Hexagenia Nymph #6, #8; Michigan Spinner #6, #8; Fishfly #6, #8

Isonychia campestris
Dun Variant #10

Isonychia sicca
Pale Western Leadwing #10; Dun Variant #10

Isonychia velma
Dun Variant #10; Great Western Leadwing #8, #10; Leadwing Coachman #8, #10

Leptophlebia cupida
Leptophlebia Nymph #10, #12; Whirling Dun (Borcher's Drake, Black Quill) #12, #14

Leptophlebia gravastella
Lepto. Nymph #12; West. Black Quill #14; Whirling Dun (Borcher's Drake, Black Quill) #14

Paraleptophlebia packii
Leptophlebia Nymph #16; Dark Bl. Quill #18; West. Bl. Dun #18; Bl. Quill Spinner #14, #16

Pseudocloeon edmundsi
Tiny Western Olive #20, #22; Tiny Bluewinged Olive #20, #22

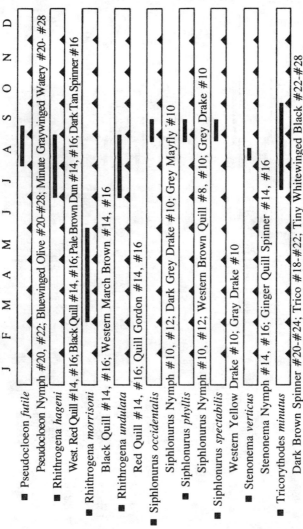

J F M A M J J A S O N D

- Pseudocloeon *futile*
  Pseudocloeon Nymph #20, #22; Bluewinged Olive #20-#28; Minute Graywinged Watery #20- #28
- Rhithrogena *hageni*
  West. Red Quill #14, #16; Black Quill #14, #16; Pale Brown Dun #14, #16; Dark Tan Spinner #16
- Rhithrogena *morrisoni*
  Black Quill #14, #16; Western March Brown #14, #16
- Rhithrogena *undulata*
  Red Quill #14, #16; Quill Gordon #14, #16
- Siphlonurus *occidentalis*
  Siphlonurus Nymph #10, #12; Dark Grey Drake #10; Grey Mayfly #10
- Siphlonurus *phyllis*
  Siphlonurus Nymph #10, #12; Western Brown Quill #8, #10; Grey Drake #10
- Siphlonurus *spectabilis*
  Western Yellow Drake #10; Gray Drake #10
- Stenonema *verticus*
  Stenonema Nymph #14, #16; Ginger Quill Spinner #14, #16
- Tricorythodes *minutus*
  Dark Brown Spinner #20-#24; Trico #18-#22; Tiny Whitewinged Black #22-#28

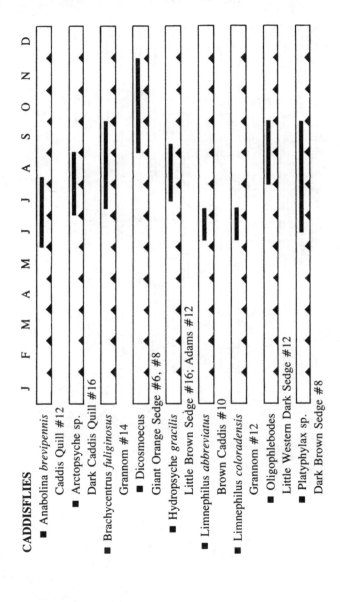

CADDISFLIES

J F M A M J J A S O N D

- *Anabolina brevipennis*
  Caddis Quill #12
- *Arctopsyche* sp.
  Dark Caddis Quill #16
- *Brachycentrus fuliginosus*
  Grannom #14
- *Dicosmoecus*
  Giant Orange Sedge #6, #8
- *Hydropsyche gracilis*
  Little Brown Sedge #16; Adams #12
- *Limnephilus abbreviatus*
  Brown Caddis #10
- *Limnephilus coloradensis*
  Grannom #12
- *Oligophlebodes*
  Little Western Dark Sedge #12
- *Platyphylax* sp.
  Dark Brown Sedge #8

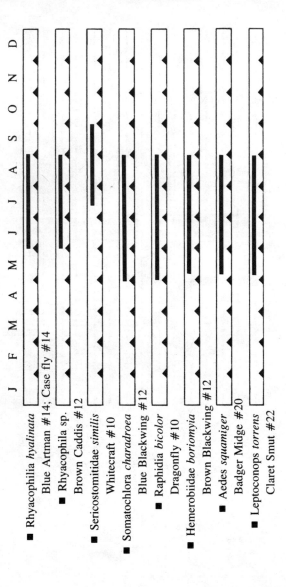

J F M A M J J A S O N D

■ Rhyacophilia hyalinata
Blue Artman #14; Case fly #14

■ Rhyacophila sp.
Brown Caddis #12

■ Sericostomitidae similis
Whitecraft #10

■ Somatochlora charadroea
Blue Blackwing #12

■ Raphidia bicolor
Dragonfly #10

■ Hemerobiidae boriomyia
Brown Blackwing #12

■ Aedes squamiger
Badger Midge #20

■ Leptoconops torrens
Claret Smut #22

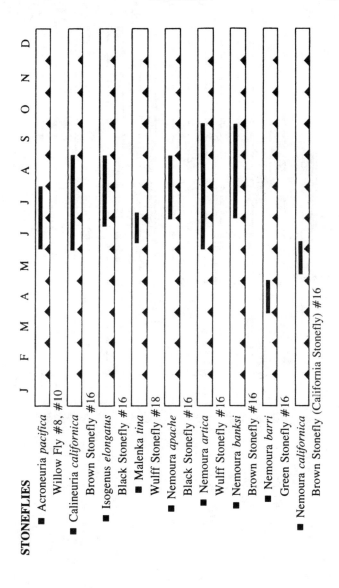

STONEFLIES

J F M A M J J A S O N D

■ Acroneuria pacifica
  Willow Fly #8, #10
■ Calineuria californica
  Brown Stonefly #16
■ Isogenus elongatus
  Black Stonefly #16
■ Malenka tina
  Wulff Stonefly #18
■ Nemoura apache
  Black Stonefly #16
■ Nemoura artica
  Wulff Stonefly #16
■ Nemoura banksi
  Brown Stonefly #16
■ Nemoura barri
  Green Stonefly #16
■ Nemoura californica
  Brown Stonefly (California Stonefly) #16

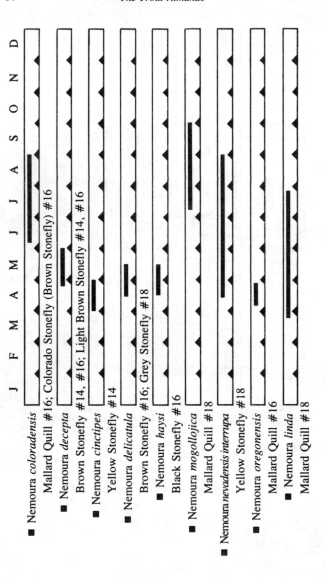

J F M A M J J A S O N D

■ Nemoura coloradensis
  Mallard Quill #16; Colorado Stonefly (Brown Stonefly) #16
■ Nemoura decepta
  Brown Stonefly #14, #16; Light Brown Stonefly #14, #16
■ Nemoura cinctipes
  Yellow Stonefly #14
■ Nemoura delicatula
  Brown Stonefly #16; Grey Stonefly #18
■ Nemoura haysi
  Black Stonefly #16
■ Nemoura mogollojica
  Mallard Quill #18
■ Nemoura nevadensis interrupa
  Yellow Stonefly #18
■ Nemoura oregonensis
  Mallard Quill #16
■ Nemoura linda
  Mallard Quill #18

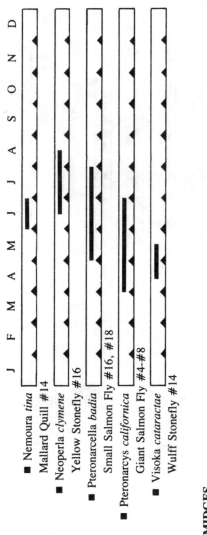

	J	F	M	A	M	J	J	A	S	O	N	D

■ *Nemoura tina*
Mallard Quill #14

■ *Neoperla clymene*
Yellow Stonefly #16

■ *Pteronarcella badia*
Small Salmon Fly #16, #18

■ *Pteronarcys californica*
Giant Salmon Fly #4-#8

■ *Visoka cataractae*
Wulff Stonefly #14

MIDGES

■ family Chironomidae
Bloodworm #18; Midge Pupa #18

■ family Empididae
Black Midge Larva #18; Black Midge #16-#22; Dun Midge #16-#22

	J	F	M	A	M	J	J	A	S	O	N	D
Sympetrum atripes												
Green Damselfly Nymph, Blue Blackwing #10, #12												
Libellula forensis												
Dragonfly Nymph #10; Western Widow Dragonfly #10, #12												
Plathemis subornata												
Dragonfly Nymph #10; Black Damselfly #10												
Sialis sp												
Alderfly Larva #12, #14; Alderfly #14												
Amphizoidae												
Black Beetle #14-#20												
order Hemiptera												
Water strider, Water bug #10-#16												
Crustaceans												
Scud, Shrimp #10-#14												
Ants												
Red Ant Black Ant #14-#18												
Grasshoppers												
Grasshoppers #8-#12												

Catch and Release ▬▬▬

Trout fishing is a sport that provides satisfaction and enjoyment to thousands of fishermen in the Rocky Mountains. Although millions of trout are bred and stocked in most of the lakes and streams in this region, there are not enough fish for everyone. For the serious trout fisherman, this problem is best solved with a catch-and-release philosophy. In many areas of Colorado and Wyoming, catch-and-release rules require that all trout be returned to the water.

Trout that are returned to the water are able to grow larger, breed future generations of trout, and provide a fishing challenge to other fishermen. In order to give the fish the best opportunity to survive the ordeal of being caught, the fisherman should follow these guidelines.

1. Use barbless hooks (required in some waters) or disarm barbed hooks by flattening the barbs with pliers.
2. Do not "play" trout to exhaustion; retrieve as quickly as possible.
3. Handle fish with wet hands and limit handling as much as possible. Contact can remove the protective "slime" on the body of the fish.
4. Avoid squeezing the fish or touching the gills.
5. Remove hooks gently. If the hook is deeply imbedded, it is better to cut the leader and leave it in the fish. Trout usually survive in these cases.
6. Exhausted trout should be revived by moving gently back and forth to push water through its gills. Release the fish in quiet water when it able to hold itself upright.

The Color of Trout ▬▬▬

Trout rarely play by the rules when it comes to coloration. Like chameleons, their body color changes with the background. Identical trout will look noticeably different after a few hours if one is placed in a black bucket of water, and one in a white bucket. In general, the main body coloration of trout will be brightest in shallow, brightly illuminated water. At the opposite extreme, the palest body colors will usually be found in deeper, darker water.

The color illustrations in this book are representitive of the major kinds of trout found in Colorado and Wyoming. Differences in habitat can produce a wide range of variation. An additional variation occurs during spawning season when male trout will be markedly brighter than females, and usually display pink-to- red flushes on their lower sides, bellies, and lower fins. The illustrations of brook and cutthroat trout show spawning colors.

Measuring Trout ━━━━━

Measure fish after placing on a flat, level surface. Body length is from the tip of the nose to the longest part of the tail.

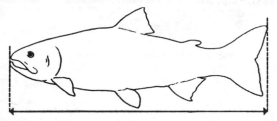

Rocky Mountain Danger

- **Rattlesnakes**. Most of the snakes found in the Rocky Mountains above 6000 feet are harmless garter snakes. Rattlesnakes aren't found above 6000 feet, and rarely above 5000 feet. At lower elevations, use common sense when in rocky terrain, and avoid putting unprotected parts of your body where you can't see, or hear, what's there.
- **Ticks**. Ticks are a seasonal problem in the Rockies, usually appearing from spring through early summer, especially after periods of wet weather. Ticks can carry a serious disease—Rocky Mountain Tick Spotted Fever—but modern medical care

provides effective treatment. The best method for dealing with ticks is frequent inspection of tight places under clothes, and immediate removal of any found. The best removal method for ticks already imbedded in the skin is to use a lit match or cigarette to force it out. Pulling on a tick may leave the head behind and result in an infection.

- **Mosquitoes and biting flies**. These universal pests have no respect for altitude; be prepared with protective clothing and repellants.
- **Giardiasis**. A microscopic organism called Giardia *lamblia* is widely distributed in water supplies in the Rocky Mountains. Even in the most remote mountain streams, it is often present, and will cause sickness if you drink the water without proper treatment (special filters, boiling, or chemicals). Symptoms occur within a few days, and include *abdominal cramps*, *diarrhea*, *fever*, and *nausea*. If you suspect that you are infected, see a physician; the treament is simple and effective.
- **Altitude sickness**. Visitors to Colorado and Wyoming may feel the effects of the altitude if they make a rapid transition from a lower elevation. Reduced oxygen is the culprit, and allowing a few days for adjustment is the best prevention. Symptoms include *diarrhea*, *fatigue*, *headache*, *nausea*, and *difficulty breathing*. Severe cases of altitude sickness require a return to lower elevations, but in most instances, it can be treated with rest, drinking plenty of liquids (avoid alcohol and caffeine), and eating foods containing sugar or sucrose.
- **Private property**. Colorado and Wyoming have long been a favorite destination for fishermen, and private landowners who don't care for their presence have generally done an adequate job of marking their territory. Local contacts, regional fishing guides, and friendly inquiries can often locate property where permission may be granted for fishing access, but always ask first. Float tubes are currently the biggest problem with trespassing. No final legal interpretation has yet been determined on the rights of water passage, and some private landowners are defending the water part of their property with barbed wire. Arrests and fines vary according to which judge is involved—the only sure defense at present is not to challenge the posting in the first place.

Premium Trout Fishing

Colorado has more than 8,000 miles of trout rivers and streams. About 158 miles of this total has been designated *Gold Medal Water*. Gold Medal classification means that the aquatic habitat is of excellent quality and the best fishing for the largest trout is usually found there. Stocking is carried out in some of these areas, and special fishing regulations may be applied to maintain the quality of the habitat. Some Colorado streams are designated *Wild Trout Water*. These areas are not stocked in order to maintain the local populations of wild trout. Both Gold Medal Water and Wild Trout Water have areas located inside private property, and permission is required to fish there. Periodic changes in stream designations may occur.

Gold Medal Water

Arkansas River (from stockyard bridge below Salida downstream to Fern Leaf Gulch)

Blue River (from Green Mountain Reservoir Dam downstream to the Colorado River)

Colorado River (from Windy Gap Reservoir downstream to the confluence of Troublesome Creek)

Frying Pan River (from Ruedi Reservoir Dam downstream to the Roaring Fork)

Gunnison River (from upper boundary of Black Canyon National Monument downstream to the confluence of the North Fork)

Rio Grande (from the upper boundary of Coller State Wildlife Area downstream to the Farmers Union Canal)

Roaring Fork River (from the Crystal River downstream to the Colorado River)

South Platte River (from Cheesman Reservoir Dam downstream to the confluence with the North Fork of the South Platte).

Wild Trout Water

Arkansas River (from below Texas Creek downstream to 1 1/2 miles above Parkdale; from Gas Creek downstream to confluence of Four Mile Creek)

Blue River (from Green Mountain Reservoir Dam downstream 2 1/2 miles)

Cache la Poudre River (from Monroe Tunnel downstream to the Poudre Valley Canal headgate; from Poudre Fish Rearing Unit downstream to the confluence of Black Hollow; from Hombre Ranch downstream to Grandpa's Bridge)

Cascade Creek (from headwaters to the Rio de Los Pinos)

Cochetopa Creek (within the Cochetopa State Wildlfie Area)

Colorado River (from the upper end of Gore Canyon downstream to town of State Bridge)

Conejos River (from Menkhaven Ranch downstream to the Aspen Glade campground)

East River (from the bridge at Roaring Judy Hatchery downstream one mile)

Emerald Lakes (in the Weminuche Wilderness Area)

Fraser River (from one mile below Tabernash downstream to one mile above Granby)

Gunnison River (from upper boundary of the Black Canyon National Monument downstream to the confluence of the North Fork)

Lake Fork of the Conejos (from headwaters to the Rock Lake outlet dam)

Laramie River (within the Cochetopa State Wildlife Area)

Middle Fork of the South Platte River (within the Tomahawk State Wildlfie Area)

North Platte River (from Routt National Forest boundary downstream to the state line)

North St. Vrain Creek (from Horse Creek downstream to Button Rock Reservoir)

Osier Creek (from headwaters to Rio de Los Pinos)

Roaring Fork River (from Holum Lake downstream to Upper Wood Creek Bridge)

South Platte River (from Beaver Creek downstream to the South Platte Arm gauging station; from Cheesman Reservoir Dam downstream to the Wigwam Club)

Tarryall Creek (from the Pike National Forest boundary downstream to the South Platte)

Trappers Lake (in the Flattops Wilderness Area).

The Wyoming Game and Fish Department uses a periodic survey of aquatic habitat conditions to classify its streams and rivers. The latest update (completed in 1987) is oriented toward trout fishing, and the ratings reflect the productivity of each location for trout. Additional considerations used for these classifications include aesthetic qualities, accessibility, and fishing pressure.

Class 1 fisheries are considered premium trout waters, of "national importance." *Class 2* fisheries are considered very good trout waters, of "statewide importance."

Class 1 Water

Big Horn River (from Wind River Reservation Boundary to Hot Springs- Washakie County Line)

Clark's Fork of Yellowstone River (from Sunlight Creek downstream to Pat O'Hara Creek)

Green River (from below Fontennelle Reservoir downstream to Flaming Gorge Reservoir)

Middle Fork of Powder River (from mouth of canyon above Bar C ranch to Hazelton-33 Mle Road)

North Platte River (from state line downstream to Miller Creek; from below Seminoe Reservoir downstream to Pathfinder Reservoir; from Grey Reef Reservoir to Goose Egg Bridge)

Sand Creek (from mouth of Redwater through state land, including Rienecke lease; on Ranch A)

Shoshone River (from Buffalo Bill Dam downstream to Willwood Dam)

Snake River (from Jackson Lake outlet downstream to state line)

Timber Creek

Tongue River (from forest service line to fork of North and South Tongue Rivers)

Wind River (from Boysen Reservoir dam downstream about 2 miles).

Class 2 Water

Big Creek (from North Fork to mouth; from VA Hospital intake to fork of East and West Goose Creeks)

Brush Creek (from South Brush Creek downstream about 4 miles)

upper *Clark's Fork of Yellowstone River* (from state line downstream about 15 miles)

Clear Creek (from 6- Mile Ditch to fork of North and South Clear Creek)

Douglas Creek (from Pelton Creek to mouth)
Eagle Creek, East Tensleep Creek, Encampment River
Fontenelle Creek (from headwaters downstream about 12 miles)
Forty Rod Creek
Green River (from USFS boundary to Wagon Creek; from Fontenelle Reservoir to New Fork River)
Greys River (from headwaters downstream to Snake River)
Hams Fork River (from Kemmerer to Kemmerer Reservoir)
Little Bighorn River (from state line to Dayton Gulch)
Little Popo Agie River (from headwaters downstream to confluence with Deep Creek)
Medicine Lodge Creek
Middle Popo Agie River (from headwaters downstream to confluence with Sawmill Creek)
New Fork River (from East Fork River to Pine Creek)
North Fork Powder River (from mouth of canyon to Dullknife Reservoir)
North Fork Shoshone River (from Middle Creek downstream to Shoshone River)
North French Creek
North Platte River (from Miller Creek downstream to Seminoe Reservoir)
North Popo Agie River (from headwaters downstream to mouth)
North Tongue River
Piney Creek (from confluence downstream about 8 miles)
Rock River (from below headwaters to near Arlington)
Salt River (from headwaters downstream to Snake River)
Sand Creek (in Sand Creek Country Club)
Shoshone River (above Buffalo Bill Reservoir)
Smiths Fork River, South French Creek
South Piney Creek (from forest service line to Cloud Peak Reservoir)
South Tongue River, Sunlight Creek, Thorofare Creek
Tongue River (in state public fishing area)
Wind River (from headwaters downstream to Wind River Indian Reservation boundary; from Minnesela downstream to Neiber)
Yellowstone River (from headwaters to National Park boundary) parts of *Paint Rock Creek*.

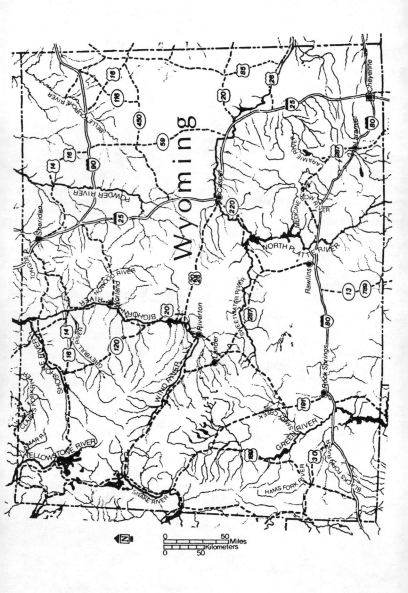

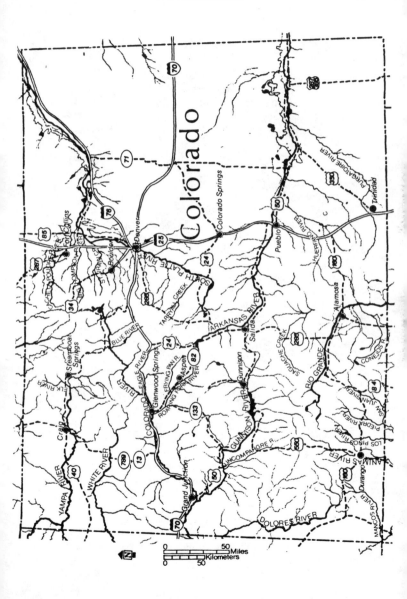

Trout Streams ━━━━━━━

Western rivers present a remarkable challenge to trout fishermen. Variations in climate and geography make these trout waters a wild mix of trickling streams and foaming rapids, silt-laden to crystal clear. The information on the following pages has been assembled to provide a picture of the seasonal variety of river conditions in Colorado and Wyoming. Streamflow and stream temperature figures were gathered from data bases assembled and maintained by the U.S. Geological Survey and various state agencies.

Waterflow information has always been recognized for its value. A territorial governor of Colorado once said, "In Colorado, water flows uphill, after money." It should be no surprise, then, to learn that this state has the distinction of being the first state to have an official water gauging station—on the Cache la Poudre River near Fort Collins, dating from April 1894. More than 75 years later, there are hundreds of gauging sites across the state, and Colorado is again leading the way with the latest technology in water measurement. A pioneer project run by the state engineer's office has added electronic links between many of the gauging sites and a satellite relay system, allowing remote, instant monitoring of streamflow conditions.

Uses for streamflow information primarily involve the value of water as a commodity, of particular importance for irrigation, municipal water supplies, and industry. Keeping an eye out for floods is also a major concern that is made more practical by measuring water conditions.

Average monthly streamflow information is similar to average weather conditions in that it represents the average water conditions found at different times of the year. The end of the snowmelt period—when dropping water levels and clearing visibility bring on the best fishing conditions—can easily be seen on the streamflow charts. Differences in snowmelt conditions created by geographical variation can also be noted by comparing charts on different pages. Not only will the peak flow vary from month to month, but the amount and percentage of change from month to month can be noted, even on separate tributaries of the same river system.

Additional clues about the nature of these rivers can be found on pages 120-125. The length of time that records have been collected from each of the gauging stations is included in this chart, along with the values known as standard deviations. These are traditional measuring units used by engineers and statisticians to place data in perspective. Average figures shown for streamflow, in this case, would be compared to the standard deviation to determine the amount of fluctuation that has occurred during the period in which the records were kept. For western rivers, this marks extreme effects from drought and above-normal precipitation.

Every attempt was made to include as many proven trout-producing areas as possible. The gauging sites included were chosen because they have been in use long enough to accumulate useful averages. Because of the fluctuations in weather from year to year in Colorado and Wyoming, recording periods of less than fifteen years are unsuitable. Also, some otherwise useful locations have had their data rendered obsolete by the construction of dams and reservoirs in the past few decades— obviously having a severe effect on streamflow.

Notes: □ *Location* is the description of the spot where the gauging station is located (U.S.G.S. uses the name of the closest town; "near" can be up to ten miles away). Additional locations are shown for some streams at sites downstream from the first location and include inflow from tributaries. In a few cases, downstream locations will have lower streamflow levels in some months, a graphic example of human intervention in the form of dams and irrigation draws. □ *Elevation* is feet above mean sea level. □ *Streamflow* is shown as mean monthly amounts in cubic feet per second. □ *Temperature* is shown as mean monthly figures in degrees Fahrenheit, from daily 24-hour averages.

Colorado Trout Streams ━━━

North Platte River
- Source: Jackson County, in Rabbit Ears Range of the Sierra Madre Mountains (area known as North Park)
- Mouth: joins South Platte River at North Platte City, Nebraska to form Platte River
- Length: 680 miles, 25 miles in Colorado
- Designation: North Platte River Drainage, Colorado Division of Wildlife Area #5
- Dams and water diversions: Lake John, MacFarlane Reservoir, Walden Reservoir

SPECIAL FISHING REGULATIONS: *Gold Medal Water*: North Platte River from southern boundary of Routt National Forest to state line. *Wild Trout Water*: North Platte River from southern boundary of Routt National Forest to state line. *Artificial flies or lures only*: North Platte River from southern boundary of Routt National Forest to state line (2 fish limit), North Platte River (in Brownlee, Manville, Peterson, Trick, Verner, Wilford State Wildlife Areas), North Fork of North Platte (in Richards State Wildlife Area).

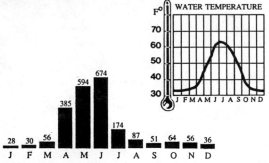

STREAMFLOW (*cubic feet per second*)
Location: near Walden   Elevation: 8000 feet

Laramie River

- Source: Larimer County, Chambers Lake in the Medicine Bow Mountains near Clark Peak
- Mouth: North Platte River at Fort Laramie
- Length: 216 miles, 27 miles in Colorado
- Designation: North Platte River Drainage, Colorado Division of Wildlife Area 5#
- Dams and Water Diversion Tunnels: diversion to Laramie-Poudre Tunnel

SPECIAL FISHING REGULATIONS: *Wild Trout Water*: Laramie River inside the Hohnholz State Wildlife Area. *Artificial flies and lures only*: Laramie River inside the Hohnholz State Wildlife Area. *Trout limit exceptions*: 2 trout limit inside Hohnholz State Wildlife Area.

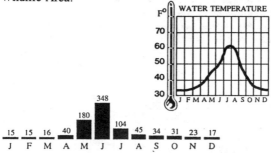

J	F	M	A	M	J	J	A	S	O	N	D
15	15	16	40	180	348	104	45	34	31	23	17

STREAMFLOW (*cubic feet per second*)
Location: near Glendevey   Elevation: 8230

North Fork of Michigan River
- Source: Jackson County, near Cameron Pass in Medicine Bow Mountains
- Mouth: merges with South Fork downstream from Gould
- Length: 7 miles
- Designation: North Platte River Drainage, Colorado Division of Wildlife Area #5

J	F	M	A	M	J	J	A	S	O	N	D
3	3	3	12	68	70	17	7	6	6	4	3

STREAMFLOW (*cubic feet per second*)
Location: near Gould   Elevation: 8793 feet

South Platte River

- Source: Park County, Pike National Forest, (area is known as South Park)
- Mouth: joins the North Platte River at North Platte City, Nebraska, forming the Platte River
- Length: 450 miles, 360 miles in Colorado
- Designation: South Platte River Drainage, Colorado Division of Wildlife Area #8
- Dams and water diversions: Antero Reservoir, Spinney Mountain Reservoir, Elevenmile Reservoir, Chatfield Reservoir, Cheesman Dam, input from Roberts Tunnel (from Dillon Reservoir), Moffat Tunnel, Adams Tunnel (Shadow Mountain Lake)

SPECIAL FISHING REGULATIONS: *Gold Medal Water*: South Platte from Cheesman Dam to confluence with North Fork, Middle Fork of South Platte from 3/4 mile above State Highway 9 bridge to lower boundary of Tomahawk State Wildlife Area.   *Wild Trout Water*: South Platte from Beaver Creek to Cheesman Reservoir, Middle Fork of South Platte inside Tomahawk State Wildlife Area.

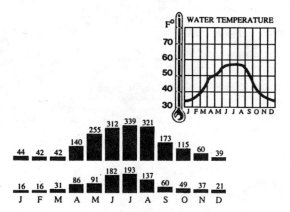

STREAMFLOW (*cubic feet per second*)
Location: above 11-Mile Canyon Reservoir near Hartsel
Elevation: 8613 feet

(Top: below Cheesman at Lake. Elevation: 6609 feet)

North Fork of South Platte River

- Source: Park County, near Whale Peak, east of Kenosha Pass
- Mouth: South Platte River at South Platte
- Length: 45 miles
- Designation: South Platte River Drainage, Colorado Division of Wildlife Area #8
- Dams and water diversions: Roberts Tunnel (input from Dillon Reservoir)

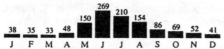

38	35	33	48	150	269	210	154	86	69	52	41
J	F	M	A	M	J	J	A	S	O	N	D

STREAMFLOW (*cubic feet per second*)
Location: below Geneva Creek at Grant   Elevation: 8561 feet

Tarryall Creek

- Source: Park County, south of Boreas Mountain, northwest of Como
- Mouth: South Platte River near Florissant
- Length: 50 miles
- Designation: South Platte River Drainage, Colorado Division of Wildlife Area #8
- Dams and water diversions: Tarryall Reservoir

SPECIAL FISHING REGULATIONS: *Wild Trout Water*: from Pike National Forest boundary downstream to confluence with South Platte River.   *Artificial flies and lures only*: Tarryall Creek from County Road 77 downstream to Ute Creek Trail Bridge
No access: no public access in North Tarryall Creek State Wildlife Area beyond 25 feet from centerline of creek.

8	7	14	50	57	136	96	64	26	20	16	11
J	F	M	A	M	J	J	A	S	O	N	D

STREAMFLOW (*cubic feet per second*)
Location: near Jefferson   Elevation: 9050 feet

North St. Vrain Creek
- Source: Boulder County, south of Long's Peak
- Mouth: South Platte River 5 miles south of Milliken
- Length: 68 miles
- Designation: South Platte River Drainage, Colorado Division of Wildlife Area #8
- Dams and water diversions: small lakes and reservoirs

SPECIAL FISHING REGULATIONS: *Wild Trout Water*: North St. Vrain from confluence with Horse Creek downstream to Button Rock Reservoir. *Artificial flies and lures only*: North St. Vrain Creek from confluence with Horse Creek downstream to inlet of Button Rock Reservoir, South St. Vrain Creek from headwaters to Brainard Lake Road (2 trout limit, 12″ or longer)
Trout limit exceptions: 2 trout on North St. Vrain Creek from confluence with Horse Creek to inlet of Button Rock Reservoir, 2 trout 12″ or longer on South St. Vrain Creek from headwaters to Brainard Lake Road.

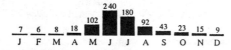

STREAMFLOW (*cubic feet per second*)
Location: North St. Vrain Creek near Allens Park
Elevation: n/a

Big Thompson River
- Source: Larimer County, Hallett Glacier in Rocky Mountain National Park
- Mouth: South Platte River southeast of Greeley
- Length: 78 miles
- Designation: South Platte River Drainage, Colorado Division of Wildlife Area #8
- Dams and water diversions: input from Alva Adams Tunnel, Mary's Lake, Lake Estes, Olympus Dam

SPECIAL FISHING REGULATIONS: *Artificial flies and lures only*: Big Thompson River from Waltonia bridge to Noel's Draw bridge. *Trout limit exceptions*: 2 trout 16″ or longer.

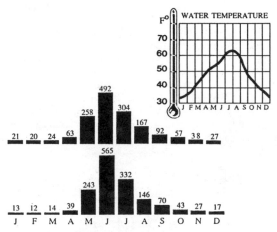

STREAMFLOW (*cubic feet per second*)
Location: Estes Park   Elevation: 7493 feet

(Top: at mouth of canyon near Drake. Elevation: 5297 feet)

Cache la Poudre River
- Source: Larimer County, Poudre Lake in Rocky Mountain National Park
- Mouth: South Platte 5 miles east of Greeley
- Length: 126 miles
- Designation: South Platte River Drainage, Colorado Division of Wildlife Area #8
- Dams and water diversions: input from Laramie-Poudre Tunnel

SPECIAL FISHING REGULATIONS: *Wild Trout Water*: Poudre River from Monroe Gravity Canal dam downstream to Poudre Valley Canal dam, Poudre River from west boundary of Hombre Ranch downstream to Grandpa's Bridge, Poudre River from Poudre Fish Rearing Unit dam downstream to Black Hollow Creek. *Artificial flies and lures only*: Poudre River from Monroe Gravity Canal dam downstream to Poudre Valley Canal dam, Poudre River from west boundary of Hombre Ranch downstream to Grandpa's Bridge, Poudre River from Poudre Fish Rearing Unit dam down-

stream to Black Hollow Creek, Poudre River from confluence with
Long Draw Creek downstream to Rocky Mountain National Park
boundary

Trout limit exceptions: 2 trout 16″ or longer on Poudre River from
Monroe Gravity Canal dam downstream to Poudre Valley Canal
dam, Poudre River from west boundary of Hombre Ranch downstream to Grandpa's Bridge, Poudre River from Poudre Fish Rearing Unit dam downstream to Black Hollow Creek.   *No fishing*:
South Fork of Poudre River from Rocky Mountain National Park
boundary downstream 1 mile.

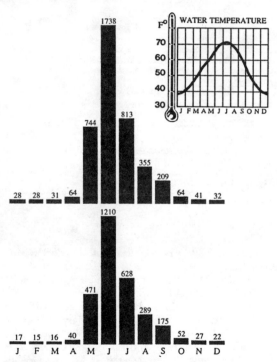

STREAMFLOW (*cubic feet per second*)
Location: near Rustic   Elevation: 7610 feet
(Top: below Elkhorn Creek. Elevation: 6448 feet)

Arkansas River

- Source: Lake County, above Leadville
- Mouth: Mississippi River near Greenville, Mississippi
- Length: 1,450 miles, 315 miles in Colorado
- Designation: Arkansas River Drainage, Colorado Division of *Wildlife Area* #1
- Dams and water diversions: input from diversions from the Eagle River, Frying Pan River, Roaring Fork River, Twin Lakes Reservoir, Turquoise Lake, Clear Creek Reservoir

SPECIAL FISHING REGULATIONS: *Gold Medal Water*: Arkansas River below Salida downstream to Fern Leaf Gulch. *Wild Trout Water*: Arkansas River below Texas Creek downstream to 1 1/2 miles above Parkdale, from confluence of Gas Creek downstream to Four Mile Creek. (See page 132 for more fishing regulations).

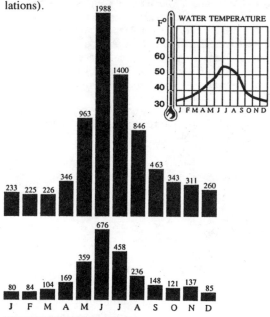

STREAMFLOW (*cubic feet per second*)
Location: near Malta   Elevation: 9300 feet
(Top: at Salida. Elevation: 7050 feet)

Colorado River

- Source: Grand County, Rocky Mountain National Park above Grand Lake
- Mouth: Gulf of California
- Length: 1,400 miles, 225 miles in Colorado
- Designation: Colorado River Drainage, Colorado Division of Wildlife Area #2
- Dams and water diversions: output to Adams Tunnel, Shadow Mountain Lake, Lake Granby, Willow Creek Reservoir, Williams Fork Reservoir, Green Mountain Reservoir, Dillon Reservoir, Ruedi Reservoir, Rifle Gap Reservoir, Morrow Point Reservoir, Blue Mesa Reservoir

SPECIAL FISHING REGULATIONS: *Gold Medal Water*: Colorado River from Fraser River downstream to confluence with Troublesome Creek. *Wild Trout Water*: Colorado River from upper end of Gore Canyon downstream to State Bridge; from lower boundary of Pioneer Park to the confluence with Troublesome Creek. *Artificial flies and lures only*: Colorado River from the lower boundary of Pioneer Park to the confluence with Troublesome Creek. *Trout limit exceptions*: 2 trout, 16″ or longer on Colorado River from the lower boundary of Pioneer Park to the confluence with Troublesome Creek

No fishing October 1—December 31: North Fork of Colorado River from Shadow Mountain Dam Spillway to Twin Creek Inlet of Lake Granby.

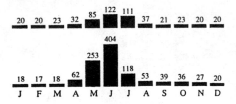

STREAMFLOW (*cubic feet per second*)
Location: near Grand Lake   Elevation: 8380 feet

(Top: below Lake Granby. Elevation: 8050 feet)

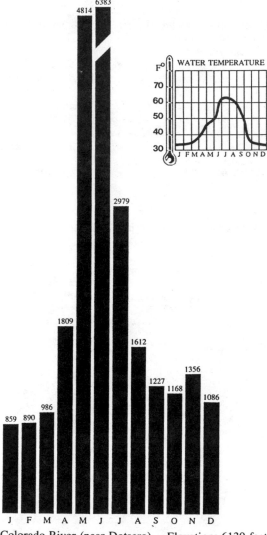

Colorado River (near Dotsero)   Elevation: 6130 feet

Willow Creek

- Source: Grand County, south of Cascade Mountain in Never Summer Mountains
- Mouth: Colorado River below Lake Granby
- Length: 25 miles
- Designation: Colorado River Drainage, Colorado Division of Wildlife Area #2
- Dams and water diversions: Willow Creek Reservoir

J	F	M	A	M	J	J	A	S	O	N	D
8	9	11	26	98	100	45	10	4	8	7	8

STREAMFLOW (*cubic feet per second*)
Location: below Willow Creek Reservoir   Elevation: 8024 feet

Fraser River

- Source: Grand County, east of Vasquez Mountains
- Mouth: Colorado River west of Granby
- Length: 40 miles
- Designation: Colorado River Drainage, Colorado Division of Wildlife #2
- Dams and water diversions: output to Moffat Tunnel

SPECIAL FISHING REGULATIONS: *Wild Trout Water*: Fraser River 1 mile below Tabernash downstream to 1 mile above Granby. (See page 134 for more fishing regulations).

WATER TEMPERATURE

J	F	M	A	M	J	J	A	S	O	N	D
40	40	50	169	447	689	219	94	62	55	54	46
7	7	7	14	53	117	48	20	13	11	10	8

STREAMFLOW (*cubic feet per second*)
Location: near Winter Park   Elevation: 8906 feet
(Top: at Granby. Elevation: 7900 feet)

Williams Fork River

- Source: Grand County, Williams Fork Mountains
- Mouth: Colorado River at Parshall
- Length: 25 miles
- Designation: Colorado River Drainage, Colorado Division of Wildlife Area #2
- Dams and water diversions: output to August P. Gumlick Tunnel, Williams Fork Reservoir

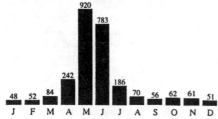

STREAMFLOW (*cubic feet per second*)
Location: below Williams Fork Reservoir   Elevation: 7615 feet

Gore Creek

- Source: Eagle County, near Vail Pass in the Gore Range
- Mouth: Eagle River at Dowds Junction
- Length: 18 miles
- Designation: Colorado River Drainage, Colorado Division of Wildlife Area #2

SPECIAL FISHING REGULATIONS: *Gold Medal Water*: Gore Creek.

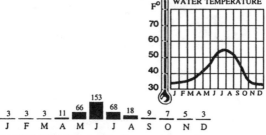

STREAMFLOW (*cubic feet per second*)
Location: near Minturn   Elevation: 8675 feet

Blue River

- Source: Summit County, Tenmile Range near Quandary Peak
- Mouth: Colorado River near Kremmling
- Length: 75 miles
- Designation: Colorado River Drainage, Colorado Division of Wildlife Area #2
- Dams and water diversions: output to Harry D. Roberts Tunnel, Dillon Reservoir, Green Mountain Reservoir

SPECIAL FISHING REGULATIONS: *Gold Medal Water*: Blue River from Green Mountain Dam downstream to Colorado River. *Wild Trout Water*: Blue River from Green Mountain Dam downstream to Colorado River. *Artificial flies and lures only*: Blue River from Green Mountain Dam downstream to Colorado River

Trout limit exceptions: 2 trout 16″ or longer on Blue River from southern boundary of Breckenridge downstream to Colorado River (except for Dillon and Green Mountain Reservoirs)

No fishing October 1—January 31: Blue River from southern boundary of Breckenridge downstream to Dillon Reservoir.

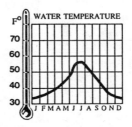

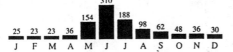

STREAMFLOW (*cubic feet per second*)
Location: near Dillon   Elevation: 9120 feet

Eagle River

- Source: Eagle County, near Tennessee Pass in Sawatch Mountains
- Mouth: Colorado River at Dotsero
- Length: 70 miles
- Designation: Colorado River Drainage, Colorado Division of Wildlife Area #2
- Dams and water diversions: output to tunnels to East Slope

SPECIAL FISHING REGULATIONS: *Trout limit exceptions*: 2 trout only on Eagle River from Gore Creek downstream to the Highway 6 bridge east of Eagle.

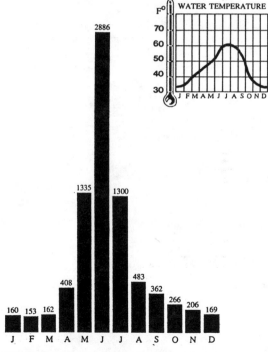

STREAMFLOW (*cubic feet per second*)
Location: at Gypsum   Elevation: 6276 feet

Roaring Fork River
- Source: Pitkin County, Independence Lake near Independence Pass in Sawatch Mountains
- Mouth: Colorado River at Glenwood Springs
- Length: 75 miles
- Designation: Colorado River Drainage, Colorado Division of Wildlife Area #2
- Dams and water diversions: output to Twin Lakes Tunnel

SPECIAL FISHING REGULATIONS: *Gold Medal Water*: Roaring Fork River from Crystal River downstream to the Colorado River.   *Wild Trout Water*: Roaring Fork River from Hallum Lake downstream to Upper Woody Creek Bridge

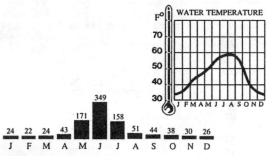

STREAMFLOW (*cubic feet per second*)
Location: near Aspen   Elevation: 8014 feet

Frying Pan River
- Source: Pitkin County, northeast of Independence Pass in the Sawatch Mountains
- Mouth: Roaring Fork River near Basalt
- Length: 40 miles
- Designation: Colorado River Drainage, Colorado Division of Wildlife Area #2
- Dams and water diversions: output to Bousted Tunnel and Carlton Tunnel, Ruedi Reservoir

SPECIAL FISHING REGULATIONS: *Gold Medal Water*: Frying Pan River from Ruedi Dam downstream to the Roaring Fork River.   (See page 134 for more fishing regulations).

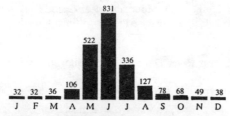

STREAMFLOW (*cubic feet per second*)
Location: Meredith   Elevation: 7780 feet

Crystal River
- Source: Pitkin County, Elk Mountains above Marble
- Mouth: Roaring Fork River near Carbondale
- Length: 40 miles
- Designation: Colorado River Drainage, Colorado Division of
  Wildlife Area #2

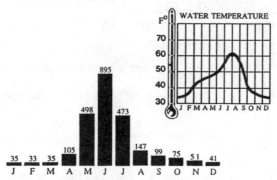

STREAMFLOW (*cubic feet per second*)
Location: Placita   Elevation: 7372 feet

Taylor River

- Source: Gunnison County, Elk Mountains near Castle Peak
- Mouth: merges with East River at Altmont to form Gunnison River
- Length: 50 miles
- Designation: Gunnison River Drainage, Colorado Division of Wildlife Area #4
- Dams and water diversions: Taylor Park Reservoir

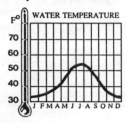

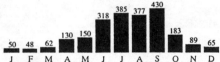

STREAMFLOW (*cubic feet per second*)
Location: below Taylor Park Reservoir   Elevation: 9170 feet

East River

- Source: Gunnison County, Emerald Lake east of Purple Mountain in Elk Mountains
- Mouth: merges with Taylor River at Altmont to form Gunnison River
- Length: 35 miles
- Designation: Gunnison River Drainage, Colorado Division of Wildlife Area #4

SPECIAL FISHING REGULATIONS: *Wild Trout Water*: East River from the bridge at the Roaring Judy fish Hatchery downstream to the Taylor River. *Artificial flies only*: East River from the upstream property boundary at the Roaring Judy Fish Hatchery downstream to the Taylor River. *Trout limit exceptions*: 8 trout 12″ or less on the East River from the upstream property boundary at the Roaring Judy Fish Hatchery downstream to the Taylor River.

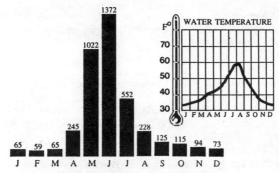

STREAMFLOW (*cubic feet per second*)
Location: Altmont   Elevation: 8006 feet

Cochetopa Creek

- Source: Saguache County, near San Luis Peak
- Mouth: Tomichi Creek near Parlin
- Length: 40 miles
- Designation: Gunnison River Drainage, Colorado Division of Wildlife Area #4
- Dams and water diversions: Lower and Upper Cochetopa Dome Reservoirs

SPECIAL FISHING REGULATIONS: *Wild Trout Water*: Cochetopa Creek within the Cochetopa State Wildlife Area. *Catch and release, artificial flies and lures only*: Cochetopa Creek inside the Coleman Ranches.

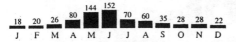

STREAMFLOW (*cubic feet per second*)
Location: near Parlin   Elevation: n/a

Gunnison River
- Source: Gunnison County, formed by merging of the Taylor River and East River at Altmont
- Mouth: Colorado River at Grand Junction
- Length: 140 miles
- Designation: Gunnison River Drainage, Colorado Division of Wildlife Area #4
- Dams and water diversions: Blue Mesa Reservoir, Morrow Point Reservoir, Crystal Dam, electrical power generation, irrigation draws

SPECIAL FISHING REGULATIONS: *Gold Medal Water*: Gunnison River from upstream boundary of the Black Canyon (Gunnison National Monument) downstream to the confluence with the North Fork of the Gunnison. *Wild Trout Water*: Gunnison River from upstream boundary of the Black Canyon (Gunnison National Monument) downstream to the confluence with the North Fork of the Gunnison. (See page 135 for more fishing regulations).

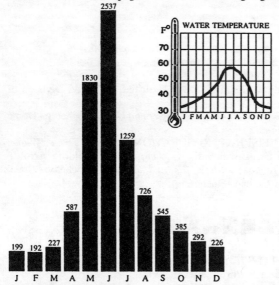

STREAMFLOW (*cubic feet per second*)
Location: near Gunnison   Elevation: 7655 feet

Uncompahgre River

- Source: San Juan County, southeast of Ironton in the San Juan Mountains
- Mouth: Gunnison River at Delta
- Length: 75 miles
- Designation: Gunnison River Drainage, Colorado Division of Wildlife Area #4
- Dams and water diversions: small storage reservoirs, input from Gunnison River diversion, Ridgeway Dam (under construction at Ridgeway)

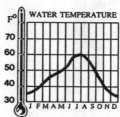

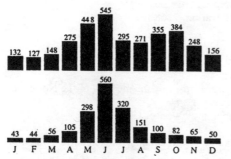

STREAMFLOW (*cubic feet per second*)
Location: near Ridgeway   Elevation: 6878 feet
(Top: at Delta. Elevation: 4926 feet)

Elk River
- Source: Routt County, west of Mount Zirkel in the Mount Zirkel Wilderness
- Mouth: Yampa River near Milner
- Length: 35 miles
- Designation: Colorado River Drainage, Colorado Division of Wildlife Area #2

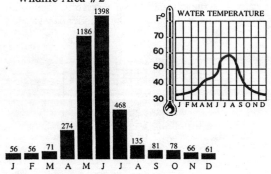

STREAMFLOW (*cubic feet per second*)
Location: Clark   Elevation: 7268 feet

Williams Fork River
- Source: Routt County, formed by the merging of the North and South Forks near Pagoda
- Mouth: Yampa River southwest of Craig
- Length: 15 miles
- Designation: Colorado River Drainage, Colorado Division of Wildlife Area #2

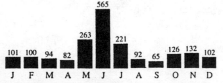

STREAMFLOW (*cubic feet per second*)
Location: Hamilton   Elevation: 6230 feet

Yampa River
- Source: Garfield County, near Derby Peak in Flattop Mountains
- Mouth: Green River near Utah state line
- Length: 180 miles
- Designation: Colorado River Drainage, Colorado Division of Wildlife Area #2
- Dams and water diversions: Stillwater Reservoir, Yampa Reservoir, Yamcollo Reservoir, Gardner Park Reservoir, Allen Basin Reservoir

SPECIAL FISHING REGULATIONS: *Trout limit exceptions*: 2 trout limit on Yampa River from Catamount Dam downstream to confluence with Elk River.

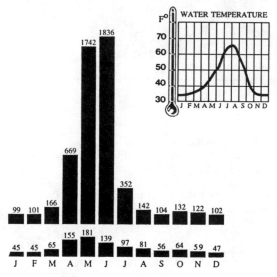

STREAMFLOW (*cubic feet per second*)
Location: near Oak Creek   Elevation: 7078 feet

(Top: at Steamboat Springs. Elevation: 6695 feet)

North Fork of White River
- Source: Garfield County, Trappers Lake in Flattop Mountains
- Mouth: merges with South Fork near Buford to form White River
- Length: 180 miles, 110 miles in Colorado
- Designation: Colorado River Drainage, Colorado Division of Wildlife Area #2

SPECIAL FISHING REGULATIONS: *No fishing*: White River from Taylor Draw Reservoir Dam (Kenney Reservoir Dam) downstream 400 yards as posted.

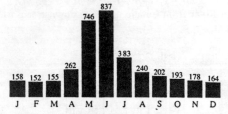

STREAMFLOW (*cubic feet per second*)
Location: near Buford   Elevation: 7010 feet

South Fork of White River
- Source: Garfield County, Flattop Mountains
- Mouth: White River below Buford
- Length: 25 miles
- Designation: Colorado River Drainage, Colorado Division of Wildlife Area #2

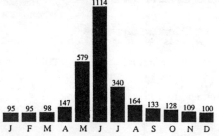

STREAMFLOW (*cubic feet per second*)
Location: near Buford   Elevation: 7480 feet

White River
- Source: Blanco County, formed by merging of North and South Forks near Buford
- Mouth: Green River at Ouray, Utah
- Length: 180 miles, 110 miles in Colorado
- Designation: Colorado River Drainage, Colorado Division of Wildlife Area #2

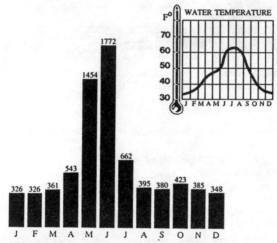

STREAMFLOW (*cubic feet per second*)
Location: below Meeker   Elevation: 5928 feet

San Juan River
- Source: Mineral County, near Wolf Creek Pass in San Juan Mountains
- Mouth: Colorado River near Rainbow Bridge National Monument
- Length: 400 miles, 55 miles in Colorado
- Designation: San Juan River Drainage, Colorado Division of Wildlife Area #7
- Dams and water diversions: Navajo Reservoir

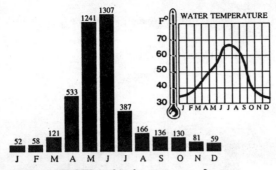

STREAMFLOW (*cubic feet per second*)
Location: Pagosa Springs   Elevation: 7052 feet

Peidra River

- Source: Mineral County, Weminuche Wilderness in San Juan Mountains
- Mouth: San Juan River at Navajo Reservoir
- Length: 45 miles
- Designation: San Juan River Drainage, Colorado Division of Wildlife Area #7
- Dams and water diversions: Williams Creek Reservoir

SPECIAL FISHING REGULATIONS: *Artificial flies and lures only*: Piedra River from the confluence with the first fork downstream to Lower Piedra Campground.

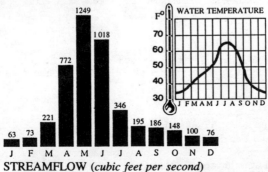

STREAMFLOW (*cubic feet per second*)
Location: near Arboles   Elevation: 6148 feet

Dolores River
- Source: Dolores County, near Lizard Head Pass in San Miguel Mountains
- Mouth: Colorado River northeast of Moab, Utah
- Length: 250 miles, 180 miles in Colorado
- Designation: Dolores River Drainage, Colorado Division of Wildlife Area #3
- Dams and water diversions: Ground Hog Reservoir, McPhee Reservoir

SPECIAL FISHING REGULATIONS: *Catch and release, artificial flies and lures only*: Dolores River from McPhee Dam downstream to Bradfield Bridge.

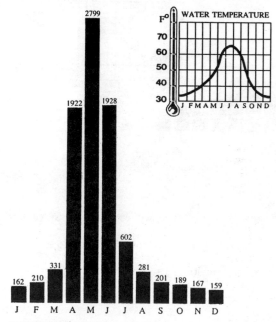

STREAMFLOW (*cubic feet per second*)
Location: Dolores   Elevation: 6919 feet

Los Pinos River
- Source: Forest County, southeast of Simpson Mountain in the Weminuche Wilderness
- Mouth: San Juan River above Navajo Dam in Navajo Reservoir
- Length: 75 miles, 60 miles in Colorado
- Designation: San Juan River Drainage, Colorado Division of Wildlife Area #7
- Dams and water diversions: Emerald Lake, Vallecito Reservoir

SPECIAL FISHING REGULATIONS: Los Pinos River within Ute Indian Reservation requires special permit. *Artificial flies and lures only*: Los Pinos River from headwaters to boundary of Weminuche Wilderness Area.

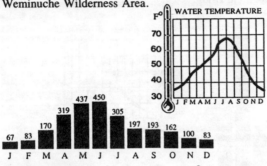

STREAMFLOW (*cubic feet per second*)
Location: La Boca   Elevation: 6144 feet

Mancos River
- Source: merger of East Mancos and West Mancos River near Mancos.
- Mouth: San Juan River south of New Mexico-Colorado border
- Length: 60 miles
- Designation: San Juan River Drainage, Colorado Division of Wildlife Area #7
- Dams and water diversions: Summit Reservoir, Puett Reservoir

STREAMFLOW (*cubic feet per second*)
Location: near Towaoc   Elevation: 5056 feet

Animas River
- Source: San Juan County, Houghton Mountain north of Eureka in San Juan Mountains
- Mouth: San Juan River at Famington, New Mexico
- Length: 110 miles, 80 miles in Colorado
- Designation: San Juan River Drainage, Colorado Division of Wildlife Area #7
- Dams and water diversions: output from Electra Lake power station

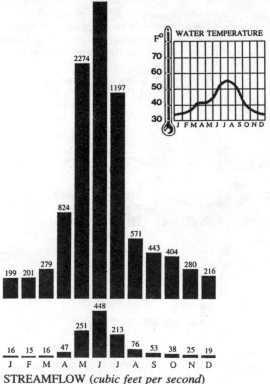

STREAMFLOW (*cubic feet per second*)
Location: Howardsville   Elevation: 9617 feet
(Top: at Durango. Elevation: 6502 feet)

Rio Grande
- Source: Hinsdale County, San Juan Mountains
- Mouth: Gulf of Mexico 22 miles east of Brownsville, Texas
- Length: 1,800 miles, 180 miles in Colorado
- Designation: Rio Grande Drainage, Colorado Division of Wildlife Area #6
- Dams and water diversions: Rio Grande Reservoir, Continental Reservoir, ouput to Rio Grande Canal

SPECIAL FISHING REGULATIONS: *Gold Medal Water*: Rio Grande from upper boundary of Coller State Wildlife Area downstream to the Farmers Union Canal. *Artificial flies and lures only*: Rio Grande from Coller Bridge downstream to the west fence of Masonic Park. *Trout limit exceptions*: 2 trout, 16″ or longer on Rio Grande from Coller Bridge downstream to the west fence of Masonic Park.

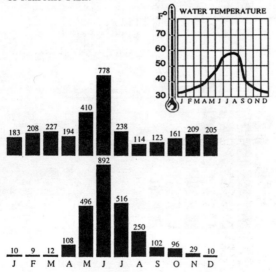

STREAMFLOW (*cubic feet per second*)
Location: Thirtymile Bridge near Creede   Elevation: 9300 feet
(Top: at Alamosa. Elevation: 7533 feet)

Conejos River

- Source: Conejos County, near Summit Peak
- Mouth: Rio Grande east of Sanford
- Length: 75 miles
- Designation: Rio Grande Drainage, Colorado Division of Wildlife Area #6
- Dams and water diverisons: Platoro Reservoir

SPECIAL FISHING REGULATIONS:*Wild Trout Water*: Conejos River from Menkhaven Ranch downstream to Aspen Glade Campground, Lake Fork of the Conejos River from headwaters downstream to the dam at the outlet of Rock Lake. *Artificial flies and lures only*: Lake Fork of the Conejos River from headwaters (including Big Lake) downstream to Rock Lake (including Rock Lake and its outlet). *Fly fishing only*: Conejos River on the Rainbow Trout Lodge property, Hamilton Ranch properties, H.E.B.O. Corporation properties, Mead Properties from Menkhaven downstream to Aspen Glade Campground. *Catch and release only*: Lake Fork of the Conejos River from headwaters (including Big Lake) downstream to Rock Lake (including Rock Lake and its outlet). (See page 136 for more fishing regulations).

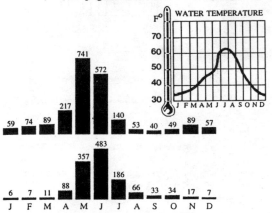

STREAMFLOW (*cubic feet per second*)
Location: Platoro   Elevation: 7800 feet
(Top: near Lasauses. Elevation: 7493 feet)

Wyoming
Trout Streams————

Gardner River
- Source: Park County, Gallatin Range in Yellowstone National Park
- Mouth: Yellowstone River near Gardner, Montana
- Length: 20 miles, 15 miles in Wyoming
- Designation: Yellowstone River Drainage, Wyoming Fishing Area #2

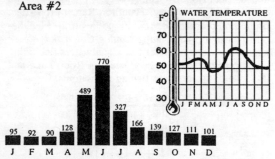

STREAMFLOW (*cubic feet per second*)
Location: near state line   Elevation: 5620 feet

Yellowstone River
- Source: Park County, southwest of Younts Peak in Absaroka Range
- Mouth: Missouri River near Montana-North Dakota border
- Length: 671 miles, 90 miles in Wyoming
- Designation: Yellowstone River Drainage, Wyoming Fishing Area #2
- Dams and water diversions: Yellowstone Lake

SPECIAL FISHING REGULATIONS: A state fishing license is not required within Yellowstone National Park, but a park fishing permit (no fee) must be obtained (see page 147).

Salmo gairdneri
RAINBOW TROUT

Salmo *trutta*
BROWN TROUT

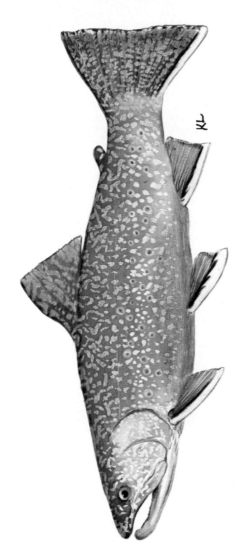

Salvelinus fontinalis
BROOK TROUT

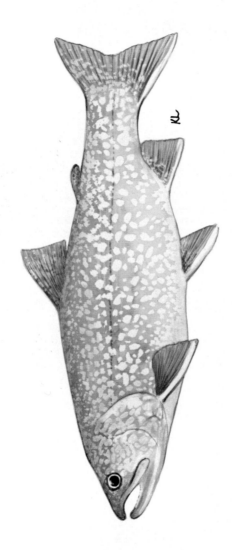

Salvelinus namaycush
LAKE TROUT

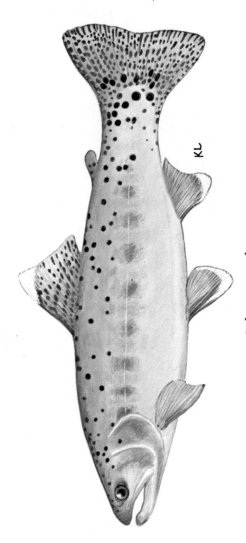

KL

Salmo *aguabonita*
GOLDEN TROUT

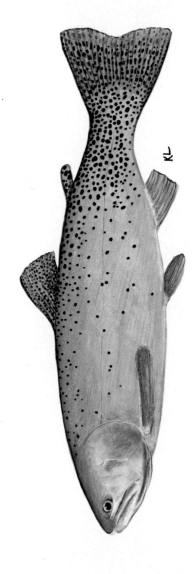

Salmo clarkii pleuriticus

COLORADO CUTTHROAT TROUT

Salmo clarki
SNAKE RIVER CUTTHROAT TROUT

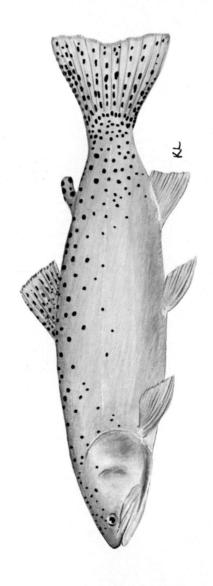

Salmo clarkii lewisi

YELLOWSTONE CUTTHROAT TROUT

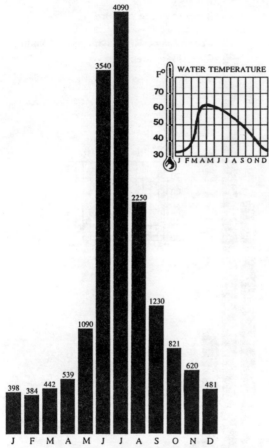

STREAMFLOW (*cubic feet per second*)
Yellowstone River (at Yellowstone Lake outlet)
Elevation: 7728 feet

Lamar River
- Source: Park County, west of Lamar Mountain at east boundary of Yellowstone National Park
- Mouth: Yellowstone River at Tower Junction
- Length: 35 miles
- Designation: Yellowstone River Drainage, Wyoming Fishing Area #2

WATER TEMPERATURE

STREAMFLOW (*cubic feet per second*)
Location: near Tower Falls Ranger Station   Elevation: 5910 feet

Wind River

- Source: Fremont County, east of Togwotee Pass
- Mouth: just downstream Wind River Canyon (south of Thermopolis) the river name changes to Bighorn River
- Length: 150 miles
- Designation: Wind River Drainage, Wyoming Fishing Area #2
- Dams and water diversions: Pilot Butte Reservoir, Boysen Reservoir, Bull Lake, Wyoming Canal of the Riverton Project, irrigation draws

SPECIAL FISHING REGULATIONS: Most of the Wind River is within the Wind River Indian Reservation, and a special permit is required (see page 149).

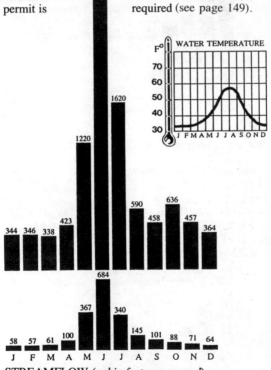

STREAMFLOW (*cubic feet per second*)
Location: near Dubois   Elevation: 7188 feet
(Top: at Riverton. Elevation: 4901)

Dinwoody Creek
- Source: Fremont County, east of Gannett Peak in Wind River Range
- Mouth: Wind River at Wilderness
- Length: 20 miles
- Designation: Wind River Drainage, Wyoming Fishing Area #2

SPECIAL FISHING REGULATIONS: Part of Dinwoody Creek is within the Wind River Indian Reservation and a special permit is required.

STREAMFLOW (*cubic feet per second*)
Location: near Burris   Elevation: 6500 feet

North Popo Agie River
- Source: Fremont County, east of Mount Washakie in Wind River Range
- Mouth: merges with Middle Popo Agie River below Lander to form Popo Agie River
- Length: 30 miles
- Designation: Wind River Drainage, Wyoming Fishing Area #2

SPECIAL FISHING REGULATIONS: *No fishing*: Middle Fork of the Popo Agie River is closed year-round from the "Rise" downstream to the bridge on the Sinks Canyon Road.

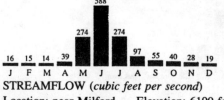

STREAMFLOW (*cubic feet per second*)
Location: near Milford   Elevation: 6190 feet

Little Popo Agie River
- Source: Fremont County, several lakes near Roaring Fork Mountain in the Wind River Range
- Mouth: Popo Agie River at Hudson
- Length: 35 miles
- Designation: Wind River Drainage, Wyoming Fishing Area #2

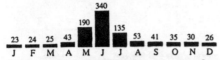

STREAMFLOW (*cubic feet per second*)
Location: near Lander   Elevation: 5436 feet

Little Wind River
- Source: merging of Sage Creek and Trout Creek near Ethete
- Mouth: Popo Agie River at Arapahoe
- Length: 15 miles
- Designation: Wind River Drainage, Wyoming Fishing Area #2

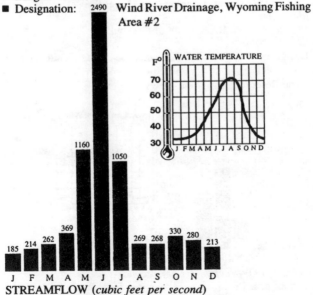

STREAMFLOW (*cubic feet per second*)
Location: near Riverton   Elevation: 4902 feet

Nowood River
- Source: Washakie County, Bighorn Mountains
- Mouth: Bighorn River at Manderson
- Length: 45 miles
- Designation: Bighorn R Drainage, Wyoming Fishing Area #2

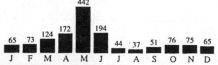

STREAMFLOW (*cubic feet per second*)
Location: near Ten Sleep   Elevation: 4420 feet

Greybull River
- Source: Park County, southeast of Mount Burwell in the Carter Mountains
- Mouth: Bighorn River south of Greybull
- Length: 70 miles
- Designation: Bighorn R Drainage, Wyoming Fishing Area #2
- Dams and water diversions: Sunshine Reservoir, Lower Sunshine Reservoir, irrigation draws

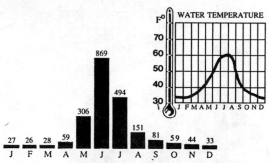

STREAMFLOW (*cubic feet per second*)
Location: near Pitchfork   Elevation: 6709 feet

Gooseberry Creek
- Source: Hot Springs County, northeast of Dome Mountain in Absaroka Range
- Mouth: Bighorn River at Neiber
- Length: 55 miles
- Designation: Bighorn R Drainage, Wyoming Fishing Area #2

2	3	6	17	47	53	13	6	6	5	4	3
J	F	M	A	M	J	J	A	S	O	N	D

STREAMFLOW (*cubic feet per second*)
Location: Dickie   Elevation: 5750 feet

Shell Creek
- Source: Big Horn County, Cloud Creek Primitive Area in Big Horn Mountains
- Mouth: Big Horn River north of Greybull
- Length: 40 miles
- Designation: Bighorn R Drainage, Wyoming Fishing Area #2
- Dams and water diversions: Shell Reservoir

SPECIAL FISHING REGULATIONS: *Trout limit exceptions*: 12 trout, only 1 longer than 20″ on Shell Creek and all waters in the eastside drainage to the Bighorn River between the state line and the confluence of Nowater Creek.

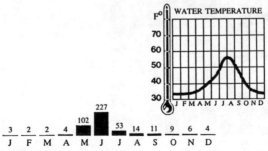

3	2	2	4	102	227	53	14	11	9	6	4
J	F	M	A	M	J	J	A	S	O	N	D

STREAMFLOW (*cubic feet per second*)
Location: above Shell Reservoir   Elevation: 9050 feet

Bighorn River
- Source: Wind River becomes Bighorn River downstream from Wind River Canyon (south of Thermopolis)
- Mouth: Yellowstone River at Bighorn, Montana
- Length: 460 miles, 110 miles in Wyoming
- Designation: Bighorn R Drainage, Wyoming Fishing Area #2
- Dams and water diversions: Boysen Reservoir, Bighorn Canal, irrigation draws

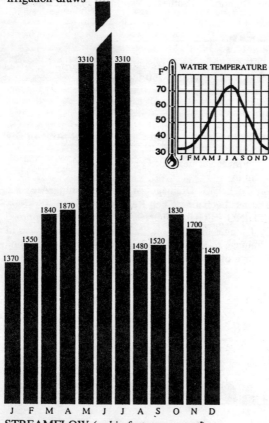

STREAMFLOW (*cubic feet per second*)
Location: Kane   Elevation: 3660 feet

Shoshone River

- Source: Park County, Buffalo Bill Reservoir (formed by merger of North Fork and South Fork of Shoshone River)
- Mouth: Bighorn Lake on Bighorn River, near Kane
- Length: 60 miles
- Designation: Shoshone R Drainage, Wyoming Fishing Area #2
- Dams and water diversions: Buffalo Bill Reservoir, storage reservoirs, Three Fork Canal diversion, Garland Canal Diversion, Corbett Dam, Willwood Dam, Mormon Dam, Penrose Dam, Heart Mountain Canal diversion, irrigation draws

SPECIAL FISHING REGULATIONS: see page 142.

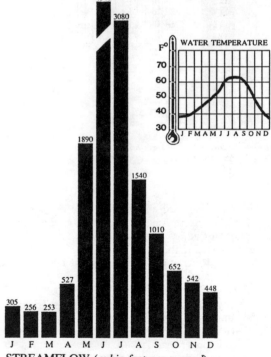

STREAMFLOW (*cubic feet per second*)
Location: below Buffalo Bill Reservoir   Elevation: 4900 feet

South Fork Shoshone River

- Source: Park County, near Crescent Mountain in Washakie Wilderness, Absaroka Range
- Mouth: Buffalo Bill Reservoir (becomes Shoshone River mainstem below reservoir)
- Length: 55 miles
- Designation: Shoshone R Drainage, Wyoming Fishing Area #2

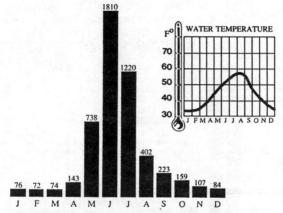

STREAMFLOW (*cubic feet per second*)
Location: near Valley   Elevation: 6200 feet

Tongue River

- Source: Sheridan County, North and South Tongue rivers merge near Burgess Junction. North Tongue River headwaters are north of Hunt Mountain in Bighorn Mountains, South Tongue River headwaters east of Granite Pass
- Mouth: Yellowstone River at Miles City, Montana
- Length: 265 miles, 35 miles in Wyoming
- Designation: Tongue R Drainage, Wyoming Fishing Area #3
- Dams and water diversions: municipal water supplies, Highline ditch, irrigation draws

SPECIAL FISHING REGULATIONS: *Trout limit exceptions*: 12 trout limit, only 1 longer than 20″ on Tongue River and all waters within the Bighorn National Forest.

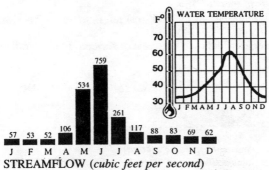

STREAMFLOW (*cubic feet per second*)
Location: near Dayton   Elevation: 4060 feet

Goose Creek
- Source: Sheridan County, Bighorn Mountains southwest of Sheridan
- Mouth: Tongue River at Acme
- Length: 60 miles, including Big Goose Creek and Little Goose Creek
- Designation: Tongue R Drainage, Wyoming Fishing Area #3
- Dams and water diversions: many small reservoirs, transbasin diversions, storage reservoirs, irrigation draws

SPECIAL FISHING REGULATIONS: *Trout limit exceptions*: 12 trout limit, only 1 longer than 20″ on Big Goose Creek and Little Goose Creek and all waters inside Bighorn National Forest.

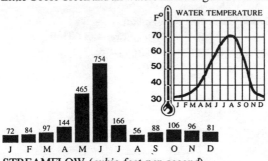

STREAMFLOW (*cubic feet per second*)
Location: near Sheridan   Elevation: 3701 feet

Middle Fork of Powder River

- Source: Johnson County, southwest of Barnum in Bighorn Mountains
- Mouth: merges with North Fork east of Kaycee to form Powder River mainstem
- Length: 30 miles
- Designation: Powder R Drainage, Wyoming Fishing Area #3

```
                 170  114
  5   5   6   28   ■    ■   20   9   8   7   6   6
  J   F   M   A   M   J   J   A   S   O   N   D
```

STREAMFLOW (*cubic feet per second*)
Location: 13 miles southwest of Barnum   Elevation: 7110 feet

North Fork of Powder River

- Source: Johnson County, west of Powder River Pass in Bighorn Mountains
- Mouth: merges with Middle Fork of Powder River east of Kaycee
- Length: 45 miles
- Designation: Powder R Drainage, Wyoming Fishing Area #3
- Dams and water diversions: Dullknife Reservoir, irrigation draws

```
                 90  87
 18  17  18  31   ■   ■  33  22  20  19  19  18
                 58  67
  2   2   2   7   ■   ■  17   7   5   4   3   3
  J   F   M   A   M   J   J   A   S   O   N   D
```

STREAMFLOW (*cubic feet per second*)
Location: above Dullknife Reservoir   Elevation: 8180 feet

(Top: 14 miles downstream from Dullknife Reservoir.
Elevation: 5590 feet)

Clear Creek

- Source: Johnson County, Bighorn Mountains west of Buffalo
- Mouth: Powder River south of Montana-Wyoming border
- Length: 75 miles
- Designation: Powder R Drainage, Wyoming Fishing Area #3
- Dams and water diversions: Cloud Peak Reservoir, Willow Park Reservoir, Kearny Lake, Lake De Smet, Kendrick Canal, irrigation draws

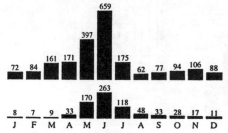

STREAMFLOW (*cubic feet per second*)
Location: near Buffalo   Elevation: 5185 feet

(Top: 2 miles upstream from mouth. Elevation: 3507 feet)

Douglas Creek

- Source: Albany County, north of Keystone in the Medicine Bow Mountains
- Mouth: North Platte River 10 miles north of Colorado-Wyoming border
- Length: 20 miles
- Designation: North Platte River Drainage, Wyoming Fishing Area #5
- Dams and water diversions: Rob Roy Reservoir, municipal water supply draws

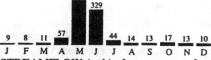

STREAMFLOW (*cubic feet per second*)
Location: near Foxpark   Elevation: 8200 feet

Encampment River
- Source: Jackson County, Colorado, near Buck Mountain in Mount Zirkel Wilderness, Sierra Madre Mountains
- Mouth: North Platte River south of Cow Creek
- Length: 40 miles, 30 miles in Wyoming
- Designation: North Platte River Drainage, Wyoming Fishing Area #5

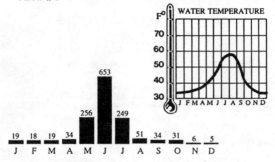

STREAMFLOW (*cubic feet per second*)
Location: 0.6 miles upstream from Hog Park Creek
Elevation: 8270 feet

North Platte River
- Source: see North Platte River, Colorado
- Mouth: joins South Platte River at North Platte City, Nebraska to form Platte River
- Length: 680 miles, 310 miles in Wyoming
- Designation: North Platte River Drainage, Wyoming Fishing Area #5
- Dams and water diversions: transbasin diversions, Seminoe Reservoir, Kortes Reservoir, Pathfinder Reservoir, Alcova Reservoirs, storage reservoirs, irrigation draws

SPECIAL FISHING REGULATIONS: *Artificial flies and lures only*: North Platte River from Wyoming-Colorado border downstream to the Saratoga Inn Bridge. *Trout limit exceptions*: 6 trout (including salmon and grayling), only 1 longer than 16″, release trout between 10-16″ on North Platte River from Wyoming-Colorado border downstream to the Saratoga Inn Bridge.

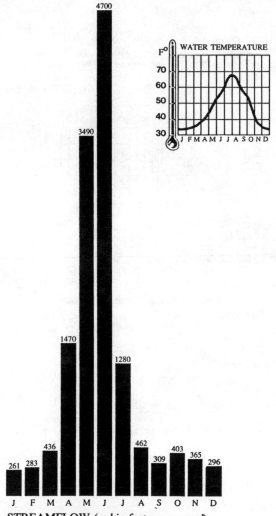

STREAMFLOW (*cubic feet per second*)
Location: Saratoga, Wyoming   Elevation: 6773 feet

Medicine Bow River
- Source: Carbon County, north of Medicine Bow Peak in Medicine Bow Mountains
- Mouth: North Platte River at Seminoe Reservoir
- Length: 195 miles
- Designation: North Platte River Drainage, Wyoming Fishing Area #5
- Dams and water diversions: irrigation reservoirs, irrigation draws

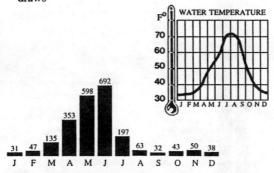

STREAMFLOW (*cubic feet per second*)
Location: 9 miles upstream from Seminoe Reservoir
Elevation: 6415 feet

Sweetwater River
- Source: Fremont County, west of Atlantic Peak in the Wind River Range
- Mouth: North Platte River at Pathfinder Reservoir
- Length: 151 miles
- Designation: North Platte River Drainage, Wyoming Fishing Area #5
- Dams and water diversions: transbasin diversion, irrigation draws

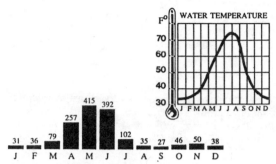

STREAMFLOW (*cubic feet per second*)
Location: 13 miles upstream from Pathfinder Reservoir
Elevation: 5920 feet

La Prele Creek
- Source: Converse County, Laramie Mountains
- Mouth: North Platte River at Orpha
- Length: 35 miles
- Designation: North Platte River Drainage, Wyoming Fishing Area #5
- Dams and water diversions: La Prele Reservoir, small reservoirs, irrigation draws

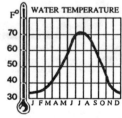

9	9	10	9	32	28	7	5	7	12	10	10
J	F	M	A	M	J	J	A	S	O	N	D

STREAMFLOW (*cubic feet per second*)
Location: near Orpha   Elevation: 4800 feet

Laramie River
- Source: Laramie County, Colorado, north of Clark Peak in Ramah Wilderness
- Mouth: North Platte River at Fort Laramie
- Length: 216 miles, 185 miles in Wyoming
- Designation: North Platte River Drainage, Wyoming Fishing Area #5
- Dams and water diversions: transbasin diversions to Cache la Poudre River (Colorado), Warren Ditch, Lake Hattie Reservoir, North Canal, Pioneer Ditch, Wheatland Reservoirs, storage reservoirs, Gering-Fort Laramie Canal, irrigation draws

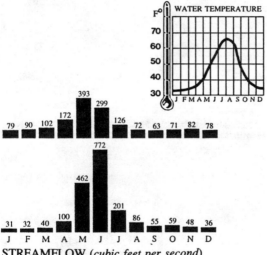

STREAMFLOW (*cubic feet per second*)
Location: Jelm   Elevation: 7683 feet
(Top: near Fort Laramie. Elevation: 4220 feet)

Green River
- Source: Sublette County, west of Gannett Peak in the Bridger Wilderness
- Mouth: Colorado River southwest of Moab, Utah
- Length: 730 miles, 230 miles in Wyoming
- Designation: Green River Drainage, Wyoming Fishing Area #4
- Dams and water diversions: Fontenelle Reservoir, storage reservoirs, irrigation draws

SPECIAL FISHING REGULATIONS: *Artificial flies and lures only*: Green River from confluence with Kendall Warm Springs downstream to the Bridger-Teton National Forest boundary. *Trout limit exceptions*: 2 trout, only 1 longer than 20", release trout between 10-20", extra brook trout limit does not apply on Green River from confluence with Kendall Warm Springs downstream to the Bridger-Teton National Forest boundary. *No fishing October 15—October 31*: Green River from Fontenelle Dam downstream to the gauge at Weeping Rocks Campground.

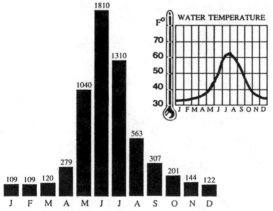

STREAMFLOW (*cubic feet per second*)
Location: 12 miles north of Daniel   Elevation: 7468 feet

New Fork River

- Source: Sublette County, west of Green River Pass in the Bridger Wilderness
- Mouth: Green River upstream from Big Piney
- Length: 60 miles
- Designation: Green River Drainage, Wyoming Fishing Area #4
- Dams and water diversions: New Fork Lakes, storage reservoir, irrigation draws

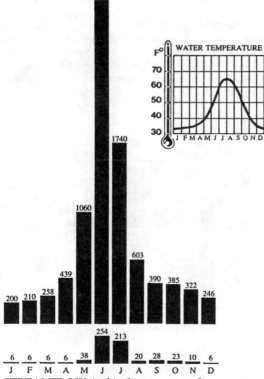

STREAMFLOW (*cubic feet per second*)
Location: 1.8 miles downstream from New Fork Lakes
Elevation: 7720 feet
(Top: 3.4 miles upstream from mouth. Elevation: 6800 feet)

Boulder Creek
- Source: Sublette County, near Raid Peak in Bridger Wilderness
- Mouth: New Fork River at Boulder
- Length: 25 miles
- Designation: Green River Drainage, Wyoming Fishing Area #4
- Dams and water diversions: Boulder Lake, irrigation draws

SPECIAL FISHING REGULATIONS: *No fishing April 1—June 30*: Boulder Creek above Boulder Lake.

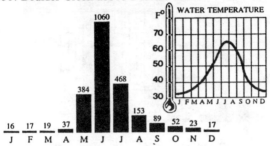

STREAMFLOW (*cubic feet per second*)
Location: 1.5 miles downstream from outlet of Boulder Lake
Elevation: 7180 feet

East Fork River
- Source: Sublette County, near Raid Peak in Bridger Wilderness
- Mouth: New Fork River south of Boulder
- Length: 35 miles
- Designation: Green River Drainage, Wyoming Fishing Area #4

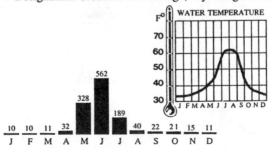

STREAMFLOW (*cubic feet per second*)
Location: near Big Sandy   Elevation: 7800 feet

Fontenelle Creek
- Source: Lincoln County, east slope of Commissary Ridge, Salt River Range
- Mouth: Green River at Fontenelle Reservoir
- Length: 40 miles
- Designation: Green River Drainage, Wyoming Fishing Area #4
- Dams and water diversions: irrigation draws

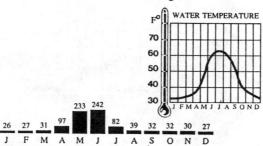

STREAMFLOW (*cubic feet per second*)
Location: 14 miles west of Fontenelle   Elevation: 6950 feet

Big Sandy River
- Source: Sublette County, north of Temple Peak in the Bridger Wilderness
- Mouth: Green River in the Seedskadee National Wildlife Refuge
- Length: 85 miles
- Designation: Green River Drainage, Wyoming Fishing Area #4
- Dams and water diversions: Big Sandy Reservoir, irrigation draws

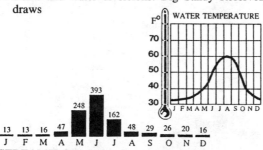

STREAMFLOW (*cubic feet per second*)
Location: near Big Sandy   Elevation: 7800 feet

Little Sandy Creek
- Source: Sublette County, east of Temple Peak in the Bridger Wilderness
- Mouth: Big Sandy River at Farson
- Length: 50 miles
- Designation: Green River Drainage, Wyoming Fishing Area #4
- Dams and water diversions: diversion to Eden No. 2 Reservoir, irrigation draws

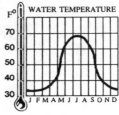

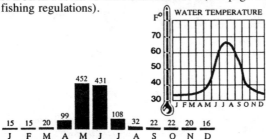

STREAMFLOW (*cubic feet per second*)
Location: 14 miles northeast of Eden   Elevation: 6750 feet

Hams Fork River
- Source: Lincoln County, west slope of Commissary Ridge in the River Range
- Mouth: Blacks Fork River at Granger
- Length: 80 miles
- Designation: Green River Drainage, Wyoming Fishing Area #4
- Dams and water diversions: Kemmerer Reservoir

SPECIAL FISHING REGULATIONS: (See page 144 for more fishing regulations).

STREAMFLOW (*cubic feet per second*)
Location: 22 miles northwest of Frontier   Elevation: 7455 feet

Henrys Fork River

- Source: Summit County, Utah, north of Gilbert Peak in the Uinta Mountains
- Mouth: Green River at Flaming Gorge Reservoir
- Length: 45 miles, 35 miles in Wyoming
- Designation: Green River Drainage, Wyoming Fishing Area #4
- Dams and water diversions: irrigation draws

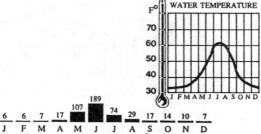

STREAMFLOW (*cubic feet per second*)
Location: 1.5 miles downstream from state line
Elevation: 8350 feet

Snake River

- Source: Teton County, near Big Game Ridge close to the southern border of Yellowstone National Park
- Mouth: Columbia River near Pasco, Washington
- Length: 700 miles, 120 miles in Wyoming
- Designation: Snake River Drainage, Wyoming Fishing Area #1
- Dams and water diversions: Jackson Lake

SPECIAL FISHING REGULATIONS: *Artificial flies and lures only*: Snake River and all tributaries (within Grand Teton National Park, except for Buffalo Fork River) from 1,000 feet below Jackson Lake Dam (at gauging station) to highway bridge at Moose. *Trout limit exceptions*: 4 trout, only 1 longer than 15″, release all trout between 11-15″ on Snake River and all tributaries (within Grand Teton National Park, except for Buffalo Fork River) from 1,000 feet below Jackson Lake Dam (at gauging station) to highway bridge at Moose. (See page 141 for more fishing regulations).

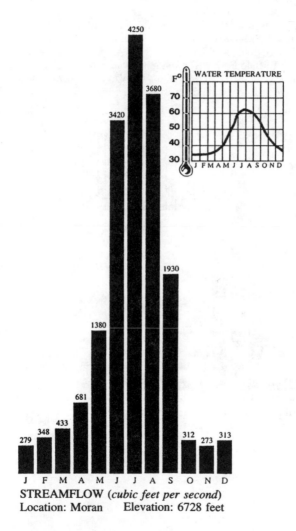

STREAMFLOW (*cubic feet per second*)
Location: Moran   Elevation: 6728 feet

Buffalo Fork River

- Source: North and South Forks headwaters in Teton County, south of Younts Peak in the Absaroka Range
- Mouth: Snake River at Moran
- Length: 15 miles, 50 miles including North and South Forks
- Designation: Snake River Drainage, Wyoming Fishing Area #1

SPECIAL FISHING REGULATIONS: *No fishing November 1—May 20*: Buffalo Fork River and other waters (exception listed on page 142) of the Snake River Drainage upstream from the Snake River Bridge at Hoback Junction.

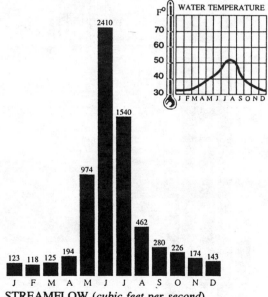

STREAMFLOW (*cubic feet per second*)
Location: near Moran   Elevation: 6773 feet

Salt River
- Source: Lincoln County, southeast of Smoot in the Salt River Range
- Mouth: Green River at Palisades Reservoir near Alpine
- Length: 50 miles
- Designation: Snake River Drainage, Wyoming Fishing Area #1
- Dams and water diversions: power developments, municipal water supply, irrigation draws

SPECIAL FISHING REGULATIONS: *No fishing November 1—December 31*: Salt River and drainage above the Upper Narrows Bridge (Wyoming Highway 238)

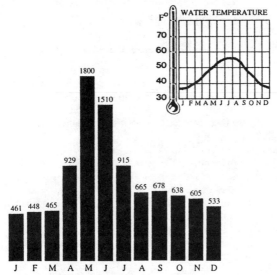

STREAMFLOW (*cubic feet per second*).
Location: 8 miles upstream from Palisades Reservoir
Elevation: 5676 feet

Weather Conditions ────

The weather information for the following locations is based on years of recorded observations from the U. S. Weather Service. In the Rocky Mountains, regional geographic features can alter local conditions drastically because of the effect of "micro-climates." Before leaving on any fishing expedition, it is wise to check local weather services for short-term predictions.

Rocky Mountain Weather Rules of Thumb ────

☞ Altitude changes temperature. Subtract 3-5.5 F.° for every 1,000 feet increase in elevation in summer months (depending on leeward or windward side of mountain). Subtract 2.2 F.° for every 1,000 feet increase in elevation in winter months.

☞ The higher the elevation, the smaller the difference between daytime and nighttime temperatures.

☞ The higher the elevation, the greater the relative humidity. This is important in maintaining warmth in winter—more difficult than at lower elevations—and cooling in summer.

☞ Precipitation increases with altitude. Rain and snow amounts will double or triple from 700 feet to 7,000 feet.

☞ Snow cover lasts longer with altitude. For every 2,000 feet increase in altitude, the period of maximum snow accumulation is a month earlier (fall) or later (spring).

☞ Major storm systems in the Rockies track from west to east with some regional variation.

☞ Temperature extremes can be local phenomenon. Cold air "pools" in shallow depressions on some slopes after sunset, causing as much as 8 F.° temperature variation between two points only 5 feet apart in elevation.

Lightning

Thunderstorms create potentially dangerous conditions. Heavy rain, hail, lightning, and wind can accompany thunderstorms. A thunderstorm moves at 5-20 miles per hour and has an average lifespan of one to two hours. These often-violent storms develop from *cumulus* clouds (flat and gray bottoms, puffy and white on top, bases 2,000-14,000 feet high). Low and thick cumulus clouds indicate a strong chance of developing into *cumulus congestus* ("cauliflower" shape, often appear in mid-to-late morning) or *cumulonimbus* clouds (the traditional thunderhead cloud, with an anvil-shaped top, often forms on the upwind side of a mountain, can grow to 3 miles wide and 3-10 miles high), which are active thunderstorm clouds. The immediate arrival of a thunderstorm is preceded by a sudden change in wind direction and speed and a drop in temperature a few minutes later. Precipitation follows the temperature drop within a few minutes and usually becomes heaviest within five minutes, dying off within 15-20 minutes.

The biggest killer in nature is lightning, which is generated during thunderstorms. Protection from lightning is best provided by shelter (buildings or vehicles). If you are stranded away from shelter:

☞ Stay away from isolated trees. Lightning seeks the most efficient grounding element (not the shortest distance), which is not always apparent. A rule of thumb: a safe distance from a tree is twice its height.

☞ If you are caught in a forest, stay within the shelter of the nearest clump of trees.

☞ Stay low to the ground (kneeling, with feet close together), in a ditch or canyon if possible, but avoid streams.

☞ If on a boat, stay low in the center of the craft.

☞ If your hair stands on end or your skin tingles, you have become a primary target for lightning and should protect yourself immediately by getting low to the ground.

☞ Avoid telephone poles, wire fences, power lines, pipelines, hilltops, open spaces.

Most people survive being struck by lightning. If someone has been struck unconscious, administer CPR, mouth-to- mouth resuscitation, or cardiac massage. Anyone who has been hit by a lightning bolt—even if not visibly harmed—should seek medical attention, as internal injuries can result.

Flash Floods ═══════════════════════

Flash floods are common in many parts of the West but are usually only dangerous to visitors away from the standard urban warning systems. Water levels in mountain streams can rise ten to twenty feet in minutes and may include walls of water that have tremendous power. Flash flooding occurs most often from heavy rain and occasionally from the breakup of ice dams. The most dangerous conditions are during prolonged periods of precipitation when the ground becomes saturated with water.

Weather authorities issue public messages about flood conditions on local television and radio stations. Standard warnings are: *Flash Flood Watch*; the possibility exists that flooding may occur soon— be prepared to take immediate action. *Flash Flood Warning*; flooding has begun or is on the verge of beginning—if in a specified area, take immediate action.

During flash flood conditions:

☞ Avoid wading in streams during flood conditions if the water is above your knees.

☞ Avoid driving through flooded areas of a road unless you are certain of the water depth. If a vehicle becomes stuck or stalls in a water crossing during flood periods, abandon it immediately—flood waves have tremendous power.

Hypothermia ═══════════════════════

Hypothermia is a condition that occurs when the human body begins to lose its core body heat. If the normal human body temperature of 98.6° is lowered by more than 10 degrees, death is almost certain. Because of the wind chill effect, hypothermia can happen even during summer months. In fact, more cases of hypothermia occur during spring and summer months than during the winter, because many fishermen, hikers, and campers are not prepared for the type of adverse weather conditions common in

the Rocky Mountains. Hypothermia can be a killer, but it is easy
to prevent.

☞ Always carry protective clothing when away from shelter; be
prepared to cover legs and add a sweater or windbreaker. If
possible, wear socks and garments that prevent sweat "wick-
ing"; perspiration is a major cause of heat loss.

☞ Symptoms: *shivering* (can become extreme and occur sporad-
ically as body temperature drops), *incoherence* (speaking is
difficult and hard to understand, thinking becomes confused),
muscle stiffness and *incoordination* (shivering will cease at
about the time stiffness sets in), *unconsciousness* (circulation
and heartbeat will slow, and victim will become unconscious
when core body temperature drops below 80°).

☞ First aid: warmth must be returned to the victim's body through
direct contact with another body, hot beverages, and external
heat sources (fire, hot bath). Once hypothermia has set in,
simply adding warm clothes or a sleeping bag will not be
enough to reverse the process. Aid should continue until all
of the symptoms have disappeared.

Wind Chill

The actual effect of wind and temperature working together
creates a lower temperature for exposed skin or any object having
a moisture content. This is because temperature drops as evapora-
tion reduces moisture. The wind chill factor—as this effect is
known—can result in dangerous conditions even when the ther-
mometer registers above-freezing temperatures.

WINDSPEED	5	10	15	20	25	30	35	40
F° **50°**	48	40	36	32	30	28	27	26
40°	37	28	22	18	16	13	11	10
30°	27	16	9	4	1	-2	-4	-5
20°	16	3	-5	-10	-15	-18	-20	-21
10°	7	-9	-18	-24	-29	-33	-35	-37
0°	-5	-22	-31	-39	-44	-49	-52	-53
-10°	-15	-34	-45	-53	-59	-64	-67	-69
-20°	-26	-46	-58	-67	-74	-79	-82	-84
-30°	-36	-58	-72	-81	-88	-93	-97	-100

Colorado Weather▬▬▬▬

Colorado is the highest state in the United States, with an average altitude of 6,800 feet above sea level. There are 54 mountains with an elevation of 14,000 feet or more and 830 mountains between 11,000 and 14,000 feet. These peaks and ranges create unique climates within the state, with local weather conditions having their greatest influence from nearby differences in elevation. The second greatest influence is the orientation of mountain ranges and valleys with respect to air movement.

These factors are best illustrated by comparing the annual snowfall at Cumbres Pass (southwest of Alamosa) with Alamosa. The former location averages 300 inches per year; the latter receives less than 29 inches. The distance between the two spots is only 50 miles.

Precipitation in Colorado comes from three general directions. The western part of the state (to the Continental Divide) gets most of its moisture from the west. Precipitation is greatest in the winter months; June is the driest month. Lower valleys in the west benefit from the protection of the surrounding high elevations, and experience more moderate weather conditions throughout the year than locations in the eastern plains.

Precipitation along the Front Range (east of the Continental Divide) generally comes from the south. Spring and summer months are when the heaviest amounts will fall, usually in the form of frequent showers and thunderstorms.   At infrequent periods during the winter months, storms moving down from the north can connect with moist air masses from the south. These rare conditions can produce blizzards, usually confined to the eastern plains and part of the foothills of the Rocky Mountains. The interaction of these two air masses occurs mostly in fall and winter months, usually without such extreme results.

NOTES: *Daily maximum and daily minimum*: Average daily and nightly high temperatures for the period in which weather records are available. *Days of precipitation*: average number of days in the month in which there occurred .1″ or more of rain or snow. *Relative humidity*: at 11:00 AM local time. *Cloudy days*: mean number of days (sunrise to sunset) with at least 50 percent cloud cover. *Thunderstorms*: mean number of days (24 hour period) with thunderstorms. *Wind*: mean speed in mph and average direction. *First/last freeze*: freeze means occurrence of a minimum temperature of 32 ° F. or lower.

Alamosa   Elevation: 7536 feet

	J	F	M	A	M	J	J	A	S	O	N	D
Daily maximum	35	40	47	58	68	78	82	80	74	63	48	37
Daily minimum	−1	6	15	25	33	41	48	46	36	25	12	1
Days of prec.	4	4	5	5	6	5	10	11	6	5	4	4
First/last freeze						June 1			September 7			

Allenspark   Elevation: 8500 feet

	J	F	M	A	M	J	J	A	S	O	N	D
Daily maximum	35	37	40	49	59	69	76	73	66	57	44	37
Daily minimum	14	15	17	24	32	39	45	43	37	30	21	16
Days of prec.	5	4	6	6	6	5	7	8	4	3	5	5
First/last freeze						June 12		August 22				

Aspen   Elevation: 7928 feet

	J	F	M	A	M	J	J	A	S	O	N	D
Daily maximum	34	37	43	53	63	74	80	77	70	60	44	35
Daily minimum	8	10	16	24	33	39	45	44	37	28	17	9
Days of prec.	6	5	5	5	4	3	5	6	4	4	5	5
First/last freeze						June 13		August 28				

Bailey   Elevation: 7730 feet

	J	F	M	A	M	J	J	A	S	O	N	D
Daily maximum	41	44	47	56	65	76	81	78	73	63	49	43
Daily minimum	9	11	15	23	31	37	44	42	36	25	16	11
Days of prec.	1	2	4	5	6	4	9	7	3	3	2	2

Buena Vista   Elevation: 7954 feet

	J	F	M	A	M	J	J	A	S	O	N	D
Daily maximum	40	43	48	56	66	77	82	79	73	64	49	42
Daily minimum	11	14	19	26	34	41	48	45	38	29	19	12
Days of prec.	1	1	2	3	3	2	5	5	3	2	2	1

Cedaredge   Elevation: 6180 feet

	J	F	M	A	M	J	J	A	S	O	N	D
Daily maximum	38	44	52	62	72	82	88	85	78	66	50	40
Daily minimum	16	20	26	33	42	50	56	54	46	36	25	18
Days of prec.	3	3	3	3	3	2	2	3	3	3	3	3

Climax   Elevation: 11350 feet

	J	F	M	A	M	J	J	A	S	O	N	D
Daily maximum	24	26	30	38	47	58	64	62	56	46	33	27
Daily minimum	3	4	7	14	24	33	39	37	31	22	11	5
Days of prec.	9	8	9	9	6	5	7	8	5	4	6	7

Cochetopa   **Creek**   Elevation: 8000 feet

	J	F	M	A	M	J	J	A	S	O	N	D
Daily maximum	26	31	40	53	65	76	81	78	72	61	44	30
Daily minimum	–6	–3	9	20	28	34	42	40	31	21	10	–2
Days of prec.	3	3	3	3	3	2	5	6	3	3	3	3

Colorado Springs   Elevation: 6145 feet

	J	F	M	A	M	J	J	A	S	O	N	D
Daily maximum	41	44	48	59	68	78	84	82	75	64	50	43
Daily minimum	16	19	23	33	43	51	57	56	47	37	25	19
Days of prec.	4	4	7	7	10	9	14	11	7	5	4	4
Rel. hum.	41	39	40	34	35	35	38	39	41	36	40	41
Wind speed/dir.	10NE	10N	11N	12N	12NW	11SE	10NW	9N	10SE	10NE	10NE	10N
Cloudy days	11	11	13	12	11	7	7	8	7	8	10	10
Thunderstorms				2	9	12	18	13	5	1		
First/last freeze				May 7						October 8		

Cortez   Elevation: 6177 feet

	J	F	M	A	M	J	J	A	S	O	N	D
Daily maximum	40	46	53	62	72	84	89	86	79	68	52	42
Daily minimum	13	18	24	31	39	47	55	53	45	34	24	15
Days of prec.	4	3	4	3	3	1	3	4	2	3	2	3

Crested Butte   Elevation: 8890 feet

	J	F	M	A	M	J	J	A	S	O	N	D
Daily maximum	27	31	37	46	59	70	76	74	67	57	40	30
Daily minimum	–1	0	8	18	28	34	40	38	31	23	11	0
Days of prec.	9	7	8	6	5	4	6	6	5	5	6	8
First/last freeze						June 24	July 23					

Del Norte   Elevation: 7884 feet

	J	F	M	A	M	J	J	A	S	O	N	D
Daily maximum	35	41	49	58	67	75	78	76	72	63	48	38
Daily minimum	7	12	19	27	35	42	48	47	40	31	19	9
Days of prec.	1	1	2	2	2	2	4	5	3	2	1	2

Denver Elevation: 5283 feet

	J	F	M	A	M	J	J	A	S	O	N	D
Daily maximum	43	46	50	61	70	80	87	86	78	67	53	46
Daily minimum	16	19	24	34	44	52	59	57	48	37	25	19
Days of prec.	6	6	9	9	10	9	9	8	6	6	5	5
Rel. hum.	45	44	42	38	38	39	36	37	40	36	44	45
Wind speed/dir.	9S	9S	10S	10S	9S	9S	8S	8S	8S	8S	9S	9S
Cloudy days	11	11	13	13	13	8	6	7	7	8	10	10
Thunderstorms				1	6	10	11	8	3	1		
First/last freeze					May 5					October 12		

Durango Elevation: 6550 feet

	J	F	M	A	M	J	J	A	S	O	N	D
Daily maximum	41	47	53	62	72	82	89	84	78	68	53	43
Daily minimum	10	15	21	28	35	41	50	48	40	30	21	13
Days of prec.	5	3	4	3	3	2	4	6	3	4	3	4

Eagle Elevation: 6500 feet

	J	F	M	A	M	J	J	A	S	O	N	D
Daily maximum	34	40	47	58	69	80	86	83	76	64	47	35
Daily minimum	3	8	18	25	33	39	46	44	35	25	15	4
Days of prec.	4	3	4	3	3	3	4	4	3	3	3	3

Estes Park Elevation: 7497 feet

	J	F	M	A	M	J	J	A	S	O	N	D
Daily maximum	38	41	44	53	62	73	79	76	70	64	47	40
Daily minimum	17	18	20	26	34	41	46	44	37	30	22	18
Days of prec.	1	1	2	3	4	4	6	5	3	2	2	2
First/last freeze						June 6			September 9			

Fort Collins Elevation: 5001 feet

	J	F	M	A	M	J	J	A	S	O	N	D
Daily maximum	41	45	50	60	70	80	86	83	75	65	50	44
Daily minimum	13	19	23	33	43	51	57	56	45	35	23	17
Days of prec.	1	1	3	4	5	4	4	3	3	2	2	1
First/last freeze					May 8					October 1		

Glenwood Springs Elevation: 5820 feet

	J	F	M	A	M	J	J	A	S	O	N	D
Daily maximum	35	42	50	61	72	83	89	86	78	66	49	37
Daily minimum	12	16	23	31	38	44	51	49	41	32	22	14
Days of prec.	5	4	4	4	4	3	3	4	3	4	3	4
First/last freeze					May 17					October 2		

Grand Junction Elevation: 4855 feet

	J	F	M	A	M	J	J	A	S	O	N	D
Daily maximum	37	44	53	65	76	86	93	89	81	68	51	39
Daily minimum	17	23	30	39	49	57	64	62	53	42	29	20
Days of prec.	7	6	7	6	6	4	5	7	5	6	5	7
Thunderstorms		1	2	4	5	8	8	5	2			
First/last freeze					April 20 October 22							

Grand Lake Elevation: 8290 feet

	J	F	M	A	M	J	J	A	S	O	N	D
Daily maximum	26	30	36	47	59	69	74	72	66	55	39	29
Daily minimum	1	2	9	20	29	36	42	41	33	25	15	6
Days of prec.	5	4	4	5	6	5	5	6	4	3	3	4
First/last freeze					June 29 July 6							

Greeley   Elevation: 4653 feet

	J	F	M	A	M	J	J	A	S	O	N	D
Daily maximum	39	46	52	62	72	83	90	87	78	67	51	43
Daily minimum	11	17	23	33	43	52	58	55	45	34	22	15
Days of prec.	1	1	2	3	5	4	3	3	3	2	2	1

Green Mountain Reservoir   Elevation: 7740 feet

	J	F	M	A	M	J	J	A	S	O	N	D
Daily maximum	31	35	42	54	65	75	81	78	72	61	44	32
Daily minimum	6	7	14	24	33	39	45	43	37	28	17	8
Days of prec.	5	4	6	6	5	4	5	6	4	3	4	4

Gunnison   Elevation: 7664 feet

	J	F	M	A	M	J	J	A	S	O	N	D
Daily maximum	26	31	41	55	66	77	81	79	73	62	45	30
Daily minimum	−7	−3	10	21	29	35	42	40	31	21	10	−3
Days of prec.	3	3	2	2	2	2	4	4	3	2	2	2
First/last freeze					June 23 August 7							

Kremmling   Elevation: 7400 feet

	J	F	M	A	M	J	J	A	S	O	N	D
Daily maximum	30	33	42	55	66	76	83	79	73	62	43	30
Daily minimum	1	1	12	21	28	35	42	40	31	21	10	0
Days of prec.	3	3	4	3	4	4	5	6	4	3	3	3

Lake City   Elevation: 8670 feet

	J	F	M	A	M	J	J	A	S	O	N	D
Daily maximum	34	38	44	53	63	73	76	75	69	61	46	36
Daily minimum	–1	0	10	21	30	37	43	41	34	24	12	0
Days of prec.	4	4	4	4	4	2	7	7	4	4	4	4

Montrose   Elevation: 5830 feet

	J	F	M	A	M	J	J	A	S	O	N	D
Daily maximum	38	44	52	62	72	83	89	86	79	67	50	40
Daily minimum	13	19	25	33	42	50	56	54	45	35	24	15
Days of prec.	2	1	2	2	2	2	3	3	3	3	2	2
First/last freeze					May 8					October 8		

Pagosa Springs   Elevation: 7238 feet

	J	F	M	A	M	J	J	A	S	O	N	D
Daily maximum	38	42	48	59	68	78	83	80	74	64	49	40
Daily minimum	3	7	15	22	30	37	45	44	36	27	16	6
Days of prec.	5	4	4	3	4	2	4	6	4	4	3	4
First/last freeze					June 21 August 18							

Ouray   Elevation: 7840 feet

	J	F	M	A	M	J	J	A	S	O	N	D
Daily maximum	38	40	45	54	64	75	79	77	71	61	46	39
Daily minimum	15	17	22	29	38	45	51	50	44	34	24	17
Days of prec.	6	7	7	6	6	3	7	9	5	5	6	6

Pueblo   Elevation: 4684 feet

	J	F	M	A	M	J	J	A	S	O	N	D
Daily maximum	46	50	55	66	76	86	91	89	82	71	57	48
Daily minimum	15	20	25	37	47	56	62	60	51	38	25	18
Days of prec.	4	5	6	6	8	7	10	9	5	4	3	3
Rel. hum.	47	41	39	33	34	33	37	39	40	38	44	48
Wind speed/dir.	8W	9W	10W	10W	10SE	9SE	9SE	8W	8SE	7W	7W	8W
Cloudy days	10	10	11	11	11	6	6	7	6	7	9	9
Thunderstorms				2	6	8	12	10	3	1		
First/last freeze				April 26						October 16		

Rangely   Elevation: 5216 feet

	J	F	M	A	M	J	J	A	S	O	N	D
Daily maximum	32	40	51	63	74	85	92	89	80	67	49	35
Daily minimum	1	9	20	31	39	47	54	51	41	30	18	7
Days of prec.	2	2	2	3	3	2	2	3	2	2	2	2

Red Feather Lakes   Elevation: 8170 feet

	J	F	M	A	M	J	J	A	S	O	N	D
Daily maximum	36	38	41	48	59	70	77	74	68	58	44	38
Daily minimum	12	14	15	23	32	39	44	43	36	29	18	14
Days of prec.	3	3	4	5	5	5	7	6	3	3	3	3

Rico   Elevation: 8840 feet

	J	F	M	A	M	J	J	A	S	O	N	D
Daily maximum	38	40	43	51	61	71	77	74	68	60	47	40
Daily minimum	4	6	12	20	27	33	40	39	33	25	15	7
Days of prec.	7	6	8	6	6	4	9	9	6	6	6	7

Saguache   Elevation: 7700 feet

	J	F	M	A	M	J	J	A	S	O	N	D
Daily maximum	36	41	49	59	68	78	82	79	74	64	48	38
Daily minimum	4	10	17	24	33	41	47	45	37	27	15	6
Days of prec.	2	1	2	2	3	2	5	6	3	2	2	1
First/last freeze						June 4			September 18			

Salida   Elevation: 7060 feet

	J	F	M	A	M	J	J	A	S	O	N	D
Daily maximum	44	47	52	61	71	79	84	81	75	66	53	44
Daily minimum	14	15	20	28	36	43	48	47	38	29	20	14
Days of prec.	1	2	3	3	4	3	6	6	3	2	2	2
First/last freeze						May 31			September 12			

Silverton   Elevation: 9320 feet

	J	F	M	A	M	J	J	A	S	O	N	D
Daily maximum	34	37	40	47	58	69	74	71	66	57	44	36
Daily minimum	−1	0	7	18	27	32	38	37	31	23	10	2
Days of prec.	6	6	7	6	5	5	10	11	7	6	5	6

Steamboat Springs   Elevation: 6770 feet

	J	F	M	A	M	J	J	A	S	O	N	D
Daily maximum	29	34	41	53	65	75	83	80	72	61	43	31
Daily minimum	2	5	12	24	31	35	41	40	32	24	14	4
Days of prec.	9	7	7	6	6	4	4	4	4	4	5	8
First/last freeze						June 23	July 21					

Telluride   Elevation: 8756 feet

	J	F	M	A	M	J	J	A	S	O	N	D
Daily maximum	37	40	42	51	62	73	78	75	69	61	46	39
Daily minimum	6	8	14	22	30	36	42	41	34	26	15	8
Days of prec.	5	5	6	6	5	3	7	8	5	4	5	5
First/last freeze						June 23		August 2				

Twin Lakes Reservoir   Elevation: 9300 feet

	J	F	M	A	M	J	J	A	S	O	N	D
Daily maximum	31	34	38	45	56	67	73	70	64	53	41	32
Daily minimum	1	0	8	15	25	33	40	38	31	22	14	5
Days of prec.	2	2	3	2	3	3	4	5	3	2	2	2

Walden   Elevation: 8120 feet

	J	F	M	A	M	J	J	A	S	O	N	D
Daily maximum	27	31	37	49	61	71	78	75	68	56	40	30
Daily minimum	3	5	11	20	28	36	39	37	29	21	12	5
Days of prec.	3	2	3	3	4	3	4	6	4	3	3	3
First/last freeze						June 22	August 1					

Westcliffe   Elevation: 7860 feet

	J	F	M	A	M	J	J	A	S	O	N	D
Daily maximum	40	42	47	56	66	77	82	78	73	63	49	42
Daily minimum	6	9	16	24	32	40	44	43	35	25	15	7
Days of prec.	2	2	3	4	4	3	7	6	3	3	2	2

Yampa   Elevation: 7890 feet

	J	F	M	A	M	J	J	A	S	O	N	D
Daily maximum	31	36	41	51	63	72	78	76	68	58	43	33
Daily minimum	6	8	14	22	31	38	45	43	35	26	16	8
Days of prec.	5	4	5	6	6	5	6	7	5	4	4	5

Wyoming Weather————

Wyoming has widely varying climatic conditions, mostly created by geographic features. The mountains in the state have the greatest effect on weather and precipitation, with conditions ranging from semi-arid to heavy annual snowfall.

Most of the semi-arid conditions are east of the mountain ranges, because the prevailing westerly air movement drops most of its moisture on the western slopes. In the northwestern corner—the Yellowstone area—the highest amounts of snowfall are usually recorded (about 250 inches a year). In the Big Horn Basin, snowfall is usually less than 20 inches.

Spring and early summer generate the year's maximum precipitation. Summer rain is usually in the form of frequent showers with relatively small quantities per shower. Thunderstorms are mostly extremely local in effect, but can produce heavy rain. Winter snowfall is frequent from November through May, but rarely exceeds five inches at a time at lower elevations. Winds that produce drifting snow are usually a bigger culprit in producing winter weather problems.

Statewide precipitation events are often associated with weather patterns that create a low pressure center to the south of the state line, drawing moist warm air flow from the south. Wind is often a significant concern in Wyoming, with frequent periods in the winter months experiencing 30-40 miles per hour conditions. Gusts from 50-60 miles per hour are common.

Alton   Elevation: 6210 feet

	J	F	M	A	M	J	J	A	S	O	N	D
Daily maximum	28	33	39	50	64	72	82	80	72	60	41	30
Daily minimum	5	8	13	23	32	37	41	40	33	25	16	7
Days of prec.	6	5	4	5	6	6	3	3	3	4	4	5
First/last freeze						June 27 July 15						

Alta   Elevation: 6430 feet

	J	F	M	A	M	J	J	A	S	O	N	D
Daily maximum	29	35	39	48	62	70	80	78	69	57	40	31
Daily minimum	9	12	15	25	34	41	47	45	37	29	18	11
Days of prec.	7	5	5	6	7	8	3	4	4	5	6	6

Arvada Elevation: 3680 feet

	J	F	M	A	M	J	J	A	S	O	N	D
Daily maximum	32	39	46	59	70	80	91	90	77	65	46	35
Daily minimum	5	12	20	30	40	49	54	52	41	31	19	9
Days of prec.	2	2	2	3	5	6	3	2	3	3	2	2

Basin Elevation: 3837 feet

	J	F	M	A	M	J	J	A	S	O	N	D
Daily maximum	29	39	50	62	73	83	92	89	78	65	45	34
Daily minimum	2	11	21	31	42	50	55	52	42	31	18	8
Days of prec.	1	0	1	2	3	3	1	1	2	1	1	1
First/last freeze					May 12				September 25			

Casper Elevation: 5338 feet

	J	F	M	A	M	J	J	A	S	O	N	D
Daily maximum	33	38	43	56	66	76	87	86	74	61	45	36
Daily minimum	13	16	19	30	39	47	55	54	43	34	23	16
Days of prec.	7	8	9	10	10	8	7	5	7	6	7	7
Rel. hum.	59	57	53	50	44	41	32	31	38	46	55	59
Wind speed/dir.	17SW	15SW	14SW	13SW	12SW	11SW	10SW	10SW	11SW	12SW	15SW	16SW
Cloudy Days	17	14	16	15	14	9	5	7	8	11	14	15
Thunderstorms			‐		1	6	8	9	6	3		
First/last freeze					May 18				September 25			

Cheyenne Elevation: 6126 feet

	J	F	M	A	M	J	J	A	S	O	N	D
Daily maximum	38	41	44	55	65	74	84	82	73	62	48	40
Daily minimum	15	17	20	30	40	48	55	53	44	34	24	18
Days of prec.	6	6	10	10	12	11	11	9	7	5	6	5
Rel. hum.	44	44	45	41	39	40	34	33	37	37	42	44
Wind speed/dir.	16NW	15W	15NW	15NW	13NW	12NW	11NW	11W	12W	13W	14NW	15NW
Cloudy Days	13	12	14	14	14	9	6	8	8	9	11	13
Thunderstorms				2	8	11	13	10	4	1		
First/last freeze					May 20				Sep. 27			

Cody Elevation: 4990 feet

	J	F	M	A	M	J	J	A	S	O	N	D
Daily maximum	35	41	46	56	67	76	85	83	73	62	46	39
Daily minimum	11	17	21	31	41	49	54	53	43	35	23	16
Days of prec.	1	1	2	3	4	4	3	2	2	2	1	1

Dixon   Elevation: 6360 feet

	J	F	M	A	M	J	J	A	S	O	N	D
Daily maximum	32	36	43	55	67	76	83	81	72	61	44	35
Daily minimum	4	7	16	26	34	41	47	45	35	26	16	5
Days of prec.	3	2	3	3	3	3	3	3	3	3	3	4
First/last freeze						June 10			September 1			

Dubois   Elevation: 6917 feet

	J	F	M	A	M	J	J	A	S	O	N	D
Daily maximum	33	37	41	49	61	70	79	78	67	58	43	36
Daily minimum	9	12	14	23	31	38	42	40	32	26	17	12
Days of prec.	1	1	2	3	4	5	2	3	3	2	1	1

Encampment   Elevation: 7387 feet

	J	F	M	A	M	J	J	A	S	O	N	D
Daily maximum	33	36	41	52	64	73	81	79	71	61	45	36
Daily minimum	11	13	16	25	34	41	47	46	37	28	18	13
Days of prec.	3	2	4	5	5	4	4	4	3	3	3	3

Evanston   Elevation: 6780 feet

	J	F	M	A	M	J	J	A	S	O	N	D
Daily maximum	31	35	40	51	63	73	83	80	72	60	43	34
Daily minimum	6	8	14	23	32	38	44	42	34	25	15	8
Days of prec.	2	2	3	3	3	3	2	3	2	3	2	2
First/last freeze						June 18	August 6					

Farson   Elevation: 6595 feet

	J	F	M	A	M	J	J	A	S	O	N	D
Daily maximum	27	31	39	53	65	74	83	81	71	59	41	29
Daily minimum	−5	−1	9	22	31	39	44	42	32	21	9	−3
Days of prec.	1	1	1	2	3	3	2	2	2	2	1	2
First/last freeze						June 17	August 14					

Foxpark   Elevation: 9045 feet

	J	F	M	A	M	J	J	A	S	O	N	D
Daily maximum	27	29	33	42	54	65	72	70	62	52	36	29
Daily minimum	6	6	9	18	26	33	37	36	30	23	13	8
Days of prec.	4	4	4	4	4	4	5	5	4	3	3	4

Gillette   Elevation: 4556 feet

	J	F	M	A	M	J	J	A	S	O	N	D
Daily maximum	32	37	43	55	66	76	87	85	74	62	44	36
Daily minimum	9	15	20	30	40	48	55	53	43	34	21	14
Days of prec.	2	2	2	4	6	6	3	3	3	3	2	2
First/last freeze					May 21				September 27			

Glenrock   Elevation: 4948 feet

	J	F	M	A	M	J	J	A	S	O	N	D
Daily maximum	37	42	47	58	69	81	90	86	77	65	48	41
Daily minimum	14	19	22	32	41	49	56	54	43	34	24	18
Days of prec.	1	1	2	4	5	4	3	2	2	3	1	1

Green River   Elevation: 6089 feet

	J	F	M	A	M	J	J	A	S	O	N	D
Daily maximum	32	38	46	56	68	78	87	84	75	63	45	35
Daily minimum	5	9	17	27	36	43	49	47	37	27	16	7
Days of prec.	1	1	2	2	3	2	1	2	2	2	1	1

Jackson   Elevation: 6244 feet

	J	F	M	A	M	J	J	A	S	O	N	D
Daily maximum	26	32	39	51	63	72	82	79	71	59	39	28
Daily minimum	5	8	14	24	31	37	40	38	31	23	16	7
Days of prec.	5	3	3	3	5	5	3	4	3	3	3	5

Kaycee   Elevation: 4660 feet

	J	F	M	A	M	J	J	A	S	O	N	D
Daily maximum	38	42	47	57	68	78	88	87	75	64	48	40
Daily minimum	6	13	18	27	37	45	50	49	39	29	18	10
Days of prec.	1	1	2	4	5	5	3	2	3	2	2	1
First/last freeze					May 30				September 7			

Lander   Elevation: 5563 feet

	J	F	M	A	M	J	J	A	S	O	N	D
Daily maximum	31	38	44	55	66	75	86	84	73	60	43	34
Daily minimum	8	13	19	30	40	47	55	54	44	33	20	12
Days of prec.	4	5	7	9	9	7	6	4	5	5	5	5
Rel. hum.	58	56	51	46	44	42	34	33	39	46	57	59
Wind speed/dir.	6SW	6SW	7SW	8SW	8SW	8SW	8SW	8SW	7SW	6SW	6SW	6SW
Cloudy Days	13	11	13	14	13	9	5	6	7	9	12	12
Thunderstorms						1	4	8	9	6	3	

Laramie   Elevation: 7266 feet

	J	F	M	A	M	J	J	A	S	O	N	D
Daily maximum	32	35	40	51	62	73	81	78	70	58	42	35
Daily minimum	9	11	15	24	33	42	48	46	37	28	17	11
Days of prec.	1	1	2	2	4	4	4	3	2	2	2	1
First/last freeze					May 29				September 9			

Lovell   Elevation: 3837 feet

	J	F	M	A	M	J	J	A	S	O	N	D
Daily maximum	29	38	47	58	70	80	89	87	74	62	44	34
Daily minimum	4	12	20	30	42	49	55	51	41	30	18	9
Days of prec.	1	1	1	2	3	3	2	2	2	1	1	1
First/last freeze					May 28				September 21			

Medicine Bow   Elevation: 6570 feet

	J	F	M	A	M	J	J	A	S	O	N	D
Daily maximum	32	35	41	54	65	76	83	81	72	60	42	34
Daily minimum	10	13	17	25	34	42	47	44	35	26	17	12
Days of prec.	1	1	2	3	4	3	3	2	2	2	2	1

Pavillion   Elevation: 5440 feet

	J	F	M	A	M	J	J	A	S	O	N	D
Daily maximum	33	40	47	58	68	77	85	83	73	61	44	35
Daily minimum	9	15	20	29	40	48	54	52	42	33	20	11
Days of prec.	1	1	1	3	4	4	2	2	2	2	1	1

Powell   Elevation: 4378 feet

	J	F	M	A	M	J	J	A	S	O	N	D
Daily maximum	32	41	48	59	70	79	88	86	74	63	45	35
Daily minimum	11	17	22	31	43	51	59	55	44	35	23	14
Days of prec.	1	1	1	1	3	4	2	2	2	1	1	0

Riverton   Elevation: 4954 feet

	J	F	M	A	M	J	J	A	S	O	N	D
Daily maximum	29	38	47	58	69	79	89	87	75	62	43	33
Daily minimum	−1	7	17	28	38	46	51	48	38	28	13	3
Days of prec.	1	1	1	3	4	3	1	1	2	2	1	1
First/last freeze					May 22				September 20			

Saratoga   Elevation: 6790 feet

	J	F	M	A	M	J	J	A	S	O	N	D
Daily maximum	33	37	42	54	66	76	84	81	72	61	44	36
Daily minimum	10	13	18	26	35	43	49	47	38	28	18	12
Days of prec.	1	1	2	3	4	2	2	3	2	2	1	1
First/last freeze						June 10		August 29				

Sheridan   Elevation: 3964 feet

	J	F	M	A	M	J	J	A	S	O	N	D
Daily maximum	34	38	43	56	66	74	86	85	73	63	46	38
Daily minimum	9	14	19	31	40	48	55	53	43	33	21	13
Days of prec.	9	9	11	11	12	11	7	6	7	7	8	9
Thunderstorms					1	5	10	10	7	3		
First/last freeze					May 21				September 21			

Thermopolis   Elevation: 4313 feet

	J	F	M	A	M	J	J	A	S	O	N	D
Daily maximum	35	43	50	61	72	82	91	89	78	66	48	39
Daily minimum	6	14	21	31	40	47	53	51	41	31	19	10
Days of prec.	1	1	2	3	5	4	2	2	2	3	2	1
First/last freeze					May 22				September 17			

Yellowstone National Park   Elevation: 6200 feet

	J	F	M	A	M	J	J	A	S	O	N	D
Daily maximum	29	34	39	49	61	70	81	79	68	56	39	31
Daily minimum	10	13	15	25	34	41	46	45	36	29	19	12
Days of prec.	5	3	4	4	6	7	4	4	4	3	3	4
First/last freeze						June 8			September 7			

Wheatland   Elevation: 4638 feet

	J	F	M	A	M	J	J	A	S	O	N	D
Daily maximum	39	44	49	60	70	81	89	87	78	64	50	43
Daily minimum	16	20	23	32	41	50	56	53	43	34	25	20
Days of prec.	1	1	2	4	5	4	3	2	2	2	1	1

Worland   Elevation: 4061 feet

	J	F	M	A	M	J	J	A	S	O	N	D
Daily maximum	28	38	47	59	70	80	89	87	75	63	44	33
Daily minimum	1	10	20	31	42	50	55	51	40	30	17	7
Days of prec.	1	1	1	2	4	3	1	1	2	2	1	1
First/last freeze					May 13				September 23			

Streamflow Standard Deviation Values

Note: *Station #* is assigned by the U.S.G.S.; *Record* is number of years data was collected from station.

COLORADO

	J	F	M	A	M	J	J	A	S	O	N	D

North Platte R. (near Walden) #06613000 Record: 25 years

| 11 | 10 | 19 | 230 | 277 | 262 | 109 | 50 | 38 | 36 | 22 | 14 |

Laramie R. (near Glendevey) #06657500 Record: 72 years

| 4 | 3 | 3 | 17 | 73 | 190 | 66 | 22 | 12 | 11 | 7 | 5 |

N. Fork Michigan R. (near Gould) #06616000 Record: 31 years

| 1 | 1 | 1 | 7 | 23 | 31 | 10 | 3 | 3 | 4 | 2 | 1 |

South Platte R. (near Hartsel) #06695000 Record: 48 years

| 8 | 8 | 20 | 87 | 95 | 139 | 138 | 94 | 51 | 34 | 18 | 9 |

South Platte R. (at Lake) #06701500 Record: 57 years

| 28 | 28 | 32 | 172 | 275 | 241 | 175 | 145 | 80 | 56 | 34 | 24 |

N. Fork South Platte R. (at Grant) #06706000 Record: 44 years

| 37 | 35 | 28 | 35 | 62 | 103 | 120 | 105 | 67 | 72 | 46 | 34 |

Tarryall Cr. (near Jefferson) #06698500 Record: 10 years

| 5 | 4 | 7 | 34 | 51 | 69 | 76 | 39 | 15 | 13 | 9 | 5 |

N. St. Vrain Cr. (near Allens Park) #06721500 Record: 5 years

| 1 | 2 | 1 | 9 | 30 | 42 | 41 | 24 | 21 | 8 | 2 | 2 |

Big Thompson R. (at Estes Park) #06733000 Record: 51 years

| 4 | 3 | 4 | 17 | 88 | 188 | 140 | 48 | 23 | 18 | 9 | 6 |

Big Thompson R. (near Drake) #06738000 Record: 41 years

| 11 | 7 | 7 | 30 | 176 | 317 | 175 | 104 | 80 | 29 | 15 | 13 |

Cache la Poudre R. (near Rustic) #06747500 Record: 12 years

| 7 | 5 | 4 | 41 | 188 | 324 | 346 | 76 | 61 | 31 | 15 | 12 |

Cache la Poudre R. (below Elkhorn Cr.) #06749000 Record: 13 years

| 6 | 6 | 6 | 17 | 294 | 435 | 487 | 117 | 67 | 14 | 10 | 9 |

Arkansas R. (near Malta) #07083700 Record: 10 years

| 32 | 35 | 84 | 80 | 154 | 343 | 232 | 144 | 82 | 69 | 82 | 47 |

Arkansas R. (at Salida) #07091500 Record: 71 years

| 39 | 37 | 41 | 136 | 327 | 594 | 692 | 286 | 152 | 104 | 65 | 40 |

Rio Grande (near Creede) #08213500 Record: 72 years

| 14 | 13 | 16 | 83 | 188 | 345 | 297 | 164 | 67 | 113 | 47 | 16 |

	J	F	M	A	M	J	J	A	S	O	N	D
Rio Grande (at Alamosa) #08223000 Record: 54 years												
	57	60	111	220	535	1103	339	186	237	258	173	77
Conejos R. (at Platoro) #08245500 Record: 17 years												
	2	2	5	44	102	179	173	97	27	38	11	3
Conejos R. (near Lasauses) #08249000 Record: 60 years												
	17	23	46	263	695	563	235	92	81	69	94	23
Colorado R. (near Grand Lake) #09011000 Record: 61 years												
	6	5	6	38	107	235	126	28	19	19	10	7
Colorado R. (below Lake Granby) #09019000 Record: 31 years												
	2	2	17	67	55	126	103	9	15	15	3	3
Colorado R. (near Dotsero) #09070500 Record: 41 years												
	235	264	303	807	1998	2698	1607	465	233	274	220	195
Willow Cr. (below reservoir) #09021000 Record: 28 years												
	3	7	13	56	145	91	21	10	6	3	1	7
Fraser R. (near Winter Park) #09024000 Record: 71 years												
	2	2	2	7	40	92	46	17	11	8	5	3
Fraser R. (at Granby) #09034000 Record: 23 years												
	7	5	11	56	158	361	178	55	41	21	12	7
Williams Fork R. (below reservoir) #09038500 Record: 29 years												
	66	68	60	36	105	262	115	67	70	60	71	61
Blue R. (near Dillon) #09046600 Record: 24 years												
	3	3	2	12	69	136	95	41	18	11	7	4
Gore Cr. (near Minturn) #09065500 Record: 27 years												
	1	1	1	5	24	47	37	8	4	3	1	1
Eagle R. (at Gypsum) #09069000 Record: 38 years												
	32	13	30	122	469	587	651	116	120	78	57	43
Roaring Fork R. (near Aspen) #09073400 Record: 17 years												
	5	4	5	13	55	140	121	18	15	14	8	6
Frying Pan R. (at Meredith) #09080100 Record: 18 years												
	8	8	11	49	214	318	184	67	31	28	14	9
Crystal R. (at Placita) #09081550 Record: 16 years												
	6	7	10	58	155	240	298	61	38	28	14	7
Taylor R. (below reservoir) #09109000 Record: 43 years												
	40	38	56	145	147	234	183	135	195	124	98	68
Cochetopa Cr. (near Parlin) #09118500 Record: 8 years												
	4	6	8	38	89	89	34	21	21	12	8	7
Gunnison R. (near Gunnison) #09114500 Record: 55 years												
	50	49	63	237	833	1203	728	210	172	138	99	80

	J	F	M	A	M	J	J	A	S	O	N	D

Uncompahgre R. (near Ridgway) #09146200 Record: 23 years

5	7	11	33	83	183	165	60	49	26	12	43

Uncompahgre R. (at Delta) #09149500 Record: 43 years

25	27	31	48	175	260	233	183	157	165	124	66

Dolores R. (at Dolores) #09166500 Record: 70 years

17	18	54	386	753	786	286	127	186	160	60	23

Yampa R. (near Oak Cr.) #09237500 Record: 21 years

11	8	24	91	113	93	79	38	27	24	13	12

Yampa R. (at Steamboat Springs) #09239500 Record: 73 years

22	23	64	258	509	801	276	65	46	55	32	23

Elk R. (at Clark) #09241000 Record: 60 years

17	16	30	163	378	475	275	63	35	38	20	18

Williams Fork R. (at Hamilton) #09249500 Record: 20 years

9	9	27	115	216	396	121	31	21	21	24	14

N. Fork White R. (near Buford) #09303000 Record: 36 years

25	21	20	77	211	320	191	63	41	35	27	25

S. Fork White R. (near Buford) #09303500 Record: 31 years

10	11	14	45	180	400	157	44	35	32	15	18

White R. (below Meeker) #09304800 Record: 20 years

49	38	44	164	433	759	326	97	90	78	54	52

San Juan R. (at Pagosa Springs) #09342500 Record: 46 years

16	15	58	258	504	824	399	120	143	153	52	23

Piedra R. (near Arboles) #09349800 Record: 19 years

24	29	135	518	766	756	339	127	209	135	67	39

Los Pinos R. (at La Boca) #09354500 Record: 30 years

27	39	125	381	507	459	310	134	131	100	84	59

Animas R. (at Howardsville) #09357500 Record: 46 years

3	3	4	24	84	147	133	37	34	24	10	4

Animas R. (at Durango) #09361500 Record: 70 years

44	45	103	343	863	1335	712	289	276	309	111	56

Mancos R. (near Towaoc) #09371000 Record: 52 years

8	16	35	108	180	113	37	53	32	64	15	10

WYOMING

Yellowstone R. (at lake outlet) #06186500 Record: 60 years

127	124	130	128	384	1030	1370	726	340	209	161	129

Lamar R. (near ranger station) #06188000 Record: 47 years

21	19	17	268	1090	1420	737	142	85	93	53	25

	J	F	M	A	M	J	J	A	S	O	N	D
Gardner R. (near state line) #06191000 Record: 34 years												
	9	8	8	40	150	272	132	35	22	18	13	10
Wind R. (near Dubois) #06218500 Record: 39 years												
	13	9	10	30	126	240	178	54	26	21	14	13
Dinwoody Cr. (near Burris) #06221400 Record: 21 years												
	4	3	3	12	60	113	106	43	40	13	7	5
N. Popo Agie R. (near Milford) #06232000 Record: 18 years												
	5	3	2	26	112	207	148	38	21	16	10	6
Little Popo Agie R. (near Lander) #06233000 Record: 38 years												
	4	5	4	13	66	166	89	18	12	8	5	4
Little Wind R. (near Riverton) #66235500 Record: 43 years												
	42	95	51	163	537	1130	721	152	206	131	72	43
Gooseberry Cr. (at Dickie) #06265800 Record: 21 years												
	1	4	4	16	30	38	10	4	6	2	2	1
Nowood R. (near Ten Sleep) #06270000 Record: 22 years												
	23	17	58	94	354	174	34	21	21	18	14	12
Greybull R. (near Pitchfork) #06274500 Record: 23 years												
	6	6	7	49	145	370	245	61	33	21	15	9
Shell Cr. (above Shell Res.) #06278300 Record: 28 years												
	1	1	1	4	63	73	37	8	8	4	2	1
Bighorn R. (at Kane) #06279500 Record: 56 years												
	576	624	572	639	1460	3280	2540	1030	689	691	548	545
Shoshone R. (below B. Bill Res.) #06282000 Record: 63 years												
	122	61	77	348	1070	1780	1210	487	422	292	454	325
S. Fork Shoshone R. (near Valley) #06280300 Record: 27 years												
	9	8	12	63	250	446	555	163	65	37	18	12
Tongue R. (near Dayton) #06298000 Record: 55 years												
	9	8	7	71	167	323	115	35	26	35	17	11
Goose Cr. (below Sheridan) #06305500 Record: 43 years												
	15	36	29	59	240	379	123	35	53	38	18	15
Middle Fork Powder R. (near Barnum) #06309200 Record: 23 years												
	1	1	2	24	59	82	10	3	3	2	2	2
N. Fork Powder R. (near Hazelton) #06311000 Record: 38 years												
	1	1	1	8	21	41	8	2	2	1	1	1
N. Fork Powder R. (near Mayoworth) #06311500 Record: 33 years												
	2	2	2	21	38	55	11	8	6	4	3	2
Clear Cr. (near Buffalo) #06318500 Record: 58 years												
	7	6	6	21	78	124	67	30	21	35	14	9

J	F	M	A	M	J	J	A	S	O	N	D

Clear Cr. (near Arvada) #06324000 Record: 48 years

| 40 | 40 | 97 | 95 | 314 | 533 | 167 | 63 | 64 | 53 | 45 | 40 |

Douglas Cr. (near Foxpark) #06621000 Record: 25 years

| 3 | 5 | 39 | 143 | 197 | 28 | 6 | 10 | 11 | 7 | 4 | |

Encampment R. (above Hog Park Cr.) #06623800 Record: 20 years

| 5 | 4 | 4 | 12 | 91 | 218 | 137 | 16 | 12 | 10 | 6 | 5 |

North Platte R. (at Saratoga) #06627000 Record: 63 years

| 58 | 69 | 160 | 692 | 1440 | 2200 | 951 | 229 | 169 | 191 | 114 | 77 |

Medicine Bow R. (above Seminoe Res.) #06635000 Record:45 years

| 12 | 56 | 97 | 220 | 508 | 415 | 213 | 59 | 41 | 29 | 22 | 17 |

Sweetwater R. (near Alcova) #06639000 Record: 15 years

| 9 | 10 | 35 | 270 | 284 | 266 | 85 | 24 | 25 | 20 | 15 | 9 |

La Prele Cr. (near Orpha) #06649500 Record: 54 years

| 4 | 5 | 7 | 6 | 69 | 67 | 11 | 9 | 9 | 14 | 7 | 5 |

Laramie R. (near Jelm) #06658500 Record: 61 years

| 9 | 9 | 12 | 45 | 169 | 413 | 144 | 33 | 22 | 22 | 15 | 10 |

Laramie R. (near Fort Laramie) #06670500 Record: 69 years

| 58 | 77 | 88 | 189 | 665 | 470 | 256 | 76 | 58 | 55 | 82 | 78 |

Green R. (near Daniel) #09188500 Record: 53 years

| 24 | 20 | 27 | 108 | 352 | 516 | 476 | 184 | 93 | 65 | 32 | 24 |

New Fork R. (near Cora) #09193000 Record: 33 years

| 3 | 3 | 3 | 3 | 40 | 43 | 57 | 13 | 28 | 20 | 6 | 3 |

New Fork R. (near Big Piney) #09205000 Record: 30 years

| 40 | 49 | 90 | 204 | 522 | 1140 | 1050 | 278 | 154 | 179 | 94 | 58 |

Boulder Cr. (below Boulder Lake) #09202000 Record: 33 years

| 15 | 18 | 22 | 25 | 192 | 264 | 235 | 73 | 52 | 42 | 22 | 18 |

East Fork R. (near Big Sandy) #09203000 Record: 46 years

| 6 | 5 | 5 | 30 | 125 | 216 | 123 | 26 | 16 | 15 | 9 | 6 |

Fontenelle Cr. (near Fontenelle) #09210500 Record: 33 years

| 6 | 5 | 9 | 48 | 115 | 134 | 48 | 16 | 11 | 7 | 6 | 6 |

Big Sandy R. (near Big Sandy) #09212500 Record: 45 years

| 5 | 5 | 6 | 31 | 83 | 154 | 97 | 26 | 15 | 12 | 7 | 6 |

Little Sandy Cr. (above Eden) #09214500 Record: 27 years

| 2 | 2 | 9 | 20 | 17 | 31 | 35 | 8 | 5 | 5 | 3 | 2 |

Hams Fork (near Frontier) #09223000 Record: 32 years

| 6 | 5 | 7 | 77 | 203 | 234 | 71 | 14 | 10 | 8 | 6 | 4 |

Henrys Fork (near state line) #09226000 Record: 29 years

| 2 | 2 | 2 | 12 | 40 | 96 | 59 | 20 | 10 | 7 | 3 | 3 |

J	F	M	A	M	J	J	A	S	O	N	D

Snake R. (near Moran) #13011000 Record: 81 years

J	F	M	A	M	J	J	A	S	O	N	D
293	485	596	910	1450	1880	1420	1470	1050	357	419	535

Buffalo Fork (near Moran) #13011900 Record: 19 years

J	F	M	A	M	J	J	A	S	O	N	D
14	22	20	50	339	699	794	194	83	51	28	17

Salt R. (above reservoir) #13027500 Record: 31 years

J	F	M	A	M	J	J	A	S	O	N	D
67	71	84	319	790	848	433	187	153	127	100	84

Fly Fishing Schools

Colorado School of Fly Fishing
Box 1848
Estes Park, Colorado 80517
303-586-8812

Columbine School of Flyfishing
4305 Highway 50
Salida, Colorado 81201
303-539-3136

Taylor Creek Fly Shop
Box 1295
Basalt, Colorado 81621
303-927-4374

Orvis Wyoming School
315 Columbine Street
Denver, Colorado 80206
303-322-5014

Books ────────────────

Tim Kelley's Fishing Guide
for Colorado and Wyoming
$9.95
Hart Publications
P.O. Box 1917
Denver, CO 80201

The Colorado Angling Guide
by Chuck Fothergill
  and Bob Sterling
$14.95
Stream Stalker Publishing
Box 1010
Aspen, Colorado 81612

The Wyoming Angling Guide
by Chuck Fothergill
  and Bob Sterling
$16.95
Stream Stalker Publishing
Box 1010
Aspen, Colorado 81612

Matching the Hatch
by Ernest G. Schwiebert, Jr.
$9.95
Stoeger Publishing Company
55 Ruta Court
South Hackensack, NJ 07606

The Compleat Angler's Catalog
by Scott Roederer
$14.95
Johnson Books
1880 South 57th Court
Boulder, Colorado 80301

*The Fly Fisherman's
Streamside Handbook*
by Craig Woods
$7.95
The Stephen Greene Press
Lexington, Massachusetts

*Game Fish of the
Rocky Mountains*
by Dr. Michel Pijoan
$6.95
Northland Press
P.O. Box N
Flagstaff, Arizona 86002

*The Trout Unlimited Book
of Basic Trout Fishing*
by Bill Cairms
$7.95
Stone Wall Press, Inc.
1241 30th Street NW
Washington, D.C. 20007
or
Trout Unlimited
P.O. Box 1944
Washington, D.C. 20013

*Aquatic Insects
and Their Imitations*
by RickHafele
  and Scott Roederer
$9.95
Johnson Books
1880 South 57th Court
Boulder, CO 80301

Fly Fishing Stores⎯⎯⎯

All Pro Fishing
633 South Santa Fe
Littleton, Colorado 80120
303-795-3473

Angler's All Ltd.
5211 South Santa Fe
Littleton, Colorado 80120
303-794-1104

Angler's Covey, Inc.
917 West Colorado Avenue
Colorado Springs, CO 80905
303-471-2984

Beaver Creek Sports
2851 North Avenue
Grand Junction, CO 81501
303-245-4353

Colorado Angler
1457 Nelson Street
Lakewood, Colorado 80215
303-232-8298

Dan's Fly Shop
Box 118
Lake City, Colorado 81235
303-944-2281

Duranglers Flies and Supplies
801 B Main Avenue
Durango, Colorado 81301
303-385-4081

Elk Trout Lodge
Box 313
Kremmling, Colorado 80405
303-724-3343

F.I. Sherman
2404 Pearl
Boulder, Colorado 80302
303-444-9315

Fothergill's Outdoor Sportsman
Box 88
Aspen, Colorado 81611
303-925-3288

Front Range Anglers, Inc.
685 D South Broadway
Boulder, Colorado 80303
303-494-1375

Gardenswartz Sporting Goods
863 Main Avenue Box 1620
Durango, Colorado 81301

Match the Hatch
254 Bridge Street
Vail, Colorado 81657
303-476-5337

Nelson Fly and Tackle
72149 Highway 40 Box 336
Tabernash, Colorado 80478
303-726-8558

Roaring Fork Anglers
2114 Grand Avenue
Glenwood Springs, CO 81601
303-945-0180

Straightline Fly & Tackle
703 Lincoln Avenue Box 3510
Steamboat Springs, CO 80477
303-879-7568

Taylor Creek Angling Services
160 Highway 82 Box 1295
Basalt, Colorado 81621
303-927-4374

The Complete Angler
8255 South Holly Street
Littleton, Colorado 80122
303-694-2387

The Fisherman's Fly
161 Virginia Drive Box 4512
Estes Park, Colorado 80517
303-586-8843

The Flyfisher Ltd.
315 Columbine Street
Denver, Colorado 80206
303-322-5014

The U.S. Angler
3609 Austin Bluffs Parkway
Colorado Springs, CO 80907
303-594-6262

Western Angler
122 West Laurel Street
Fort Collins, CO 80521
303-221-4777

H & K Sales
164 North 3rd
Laramie, Wyoming 82070

High Country Flies
75 E. Broadway Box 3432
Jackson, Wyoming 83001
307-733-7210

Jack Dennis Outdoor Shop
Jackson, Wyoming 83001
307-733-3210

Wyoming Water Fly Shop
1588 Sheridan Avenue
Cody, Wyoming 82414

Organizations ────────

Trout Unlimited
Box 1944   Washington, D.C. 20013
Membership: $15 annual

The Federation of Fly Fishers
Box 1088   West Yellowstone, Montana 59758
Membership: $20 annual

Wyoming Mileage Chart

	AFTON	BASIN	BUFFALO	CASPER	CHEYENNE	CODY	DOUGLAS	DUBOIS	EVANSTON	GILLETTE	GLENROCK	GRANGER JUNCTION	GREEN RIVER	GREYBULL	GUERNSEY	JACKSON	KEMMERER	LANDER	LARAMIE	LOVELL	LUSK	MIDWEST	MOORCROFT	MORAN JUNCTION	NEWCASTLE	PINEDALE	POWELL	RAWLINS	RIVERTON	ROCK SPRINGS	SHERIDAN	SHOSHONI	SUNDANCE	THERMOPOLIS	TORRINGTON	WHEATLAND	WORLAND
BASIN	308
BUFFALO	411	120
CASPER	353	194	112
CHEYENNE	437	372	290	179
CODY	247	61	181	214	393
DOUGLAS	403	244	161	50	129	264
DUBOIS	155	196	256	198	346	203	248
EVANSTON	121	358	418	326	357	368	377	276
GILLETTE	481	191	70	137	242	251	113	326	462
GLENROCK	378	218	136	25	158	239	29	223	352	143
GRANGER JUNCTION	142	297	357	264	296	318	316	229	61	400	290
GREEN RIVER	166	273	333	240	271	293	291	205	86	376	266	25
GREYBULL	300	8	128	201	380	53	251	204	366	198	226	305	80
GUERNSEY	464	305	223	111	98	325	61	309	393	175	91	332	308	312
JACKSON	70	238	341	284	432	177	334	85	191	412	308	207	190	230	395
KEMMERER	97	344	404	311	343	338	363	246	51	447	337	47	72	352	379	160
LANDER	230	143	203	145	271	163	195	75	216	273	169	154	130	150	256	160	201
LARAMIE	388	339	261	150	49	360	136	297	308	249	165	247	222	348	105	384	294	222
LOVELL	295	40	140	234	412	48	284	236	399	207	258	337	313	33	345	225	384	183	381
LUSK	457	297	215	104	140	318	54	302	431	157	83	370	345	305	69	387	417	248	165	338
MIDWEST	398	198	78	47	225	259	97	243	372	89	71	311	287	206	158	328	358	189	196	217	150
MOORCROFT	510	219	99	164	269	280	140	355	489	28	170	428	403	227	198	440	475	306	276	236	129	117
MORAN JUNCTION	100	208	311	254	402	147	304	55	221	382	278	237	220	200	365	30	190	130	352	195	357	298	415
NEWCASTLE	521	267	147	170	221	327	135	366	495	76	164	434	410	275	151	451	481	312	247	284	81	123	48	421
PINEDALE	120	279	339	273	356	254	324	162	156	409	299	137	113	287	385	77	105	136	307	301	378	319	436	107	442
POWELL	271	63	163	239	417	24	288	227	392	230	263	342	317	56	349	201	362	187	385	23	342	240	259	171	307	278
RAWLINS	289	267	228	117	148	288	169	200	209	253	143	147	123	275	185	285	194	124	99	307	222	164	280	255	287	207	312
RIVERTON	233	118	178	120	296	139	170	78	240	248	144	179	155	126	231	164	226	25	247	158	224	164	281	134	287	161	163	142
ROCK SPRINGS	180	260	320	225	256	280	277	192	100	361	251	39	14	267	293	177	86	117	207	300	330	271	388	207	395	100	304	108	142
SHERIDAN	395	103	35	147	325	149	196	291	454	103	171	392	368	95	258	326	439	238	296	104	250	113	132	296	180	374	127	263	213	355
SHOSHONI	255	96	156	98	276	116	148	100	263	226	122	201	177	103	209	188	248	47	245	136	201	142	259	156	265	183	141	171	22	164	191
SUNDANCE	542	252	131	197	265	311	173	387	522	81	203	460	436	259	195	473	507	339	291	269	126	149	33	447	47	469	292	313	314	421	164	292
THERMOPOLIS	288	63	123	130	309	84	180	133	295	193	155	234	209	71	241	218	281	79	277	104	234	175	222	188	270	216	108	204	55	196	159	32	255
TORRINGTON	497	337	255	144	84	358	94	342	426	207	123	364	341	345	33	427	412	289	132	378	56	191	185	397	137	418	382	218	264	326	290	242	182	274
WHEATLAND	446	303	221	110	70	324	60	308	366	173	89	305	280	310	28	393	352	254	77	343	89	156	200	363	170	365	348	158	229	266	256	207	215	239	81
WORLAND	321	30	90	164	342	91	213	166	328	160	188	267	242	38	274	251	314	112	310	71	267	168	189	221	237	249	94	237	88	229	125	65	222	33	307	273
YELLOWSTONE (E. and S. entrances)	127	113	233	267	429	52	317	82	248	299	291	264	247	105	378	57	217	157	380	99	370	311	332	27	375	134	76	282	161	234	201	169	360	136	410	378	143

Colorado Mileage Chart

	ALAMOSA	ASPEN	BOULDER	BRECKENRIDGE	BRIGHTON	BUENA VISTA	CANON CITY	CASTLE ROCK	CENTRAL CITY	COLORADO SPRINGS	CONEJOS	CORTEZ	CRAIG	CREEDE	CRIPPLE CREEK	DEL NORTE	DELTA	DENVER	DOVE CREEK	DURANGO	EAGLE	ESTES PARK	FAIRPLAY	FORT COLLINS	FORT MORGAN	GEORGETOWN	GLENWOOD SPRINGS	GOLDEN	GRAND JUNCTION
ASPEN	163																												
BOULDER	227	168																											
BRECKENRIDGE	154	100	87																										
BRIGHTON	231	179	26	98																									
BUENA VISTA	100	63	132	59	136																								
CANON CITY	139	145	142	96	134	82																							
CASTLE ROCK	203	197	57	120	49	134	85																						
CENTRAL CITY	217	144	36	63	52	119	146	92																					
COLORADO SP	163	157	97	105	89	94	45	40	102																				
CONEJOS	28	191	256	182	259	128	165	231	245	191																			
CORTEZ	194	277	392	319	396	254	302	387	382	347	222																		
CRAIG	296	157	219	146	226	197	242	236	191	251	324	349																	
CREEDE	68	201	266	192	269	138	176	261	255	221	96	170	335																
CRIPPLE CREEK	181	149	142	98	134	86	42	85	147	45	209	348	243	219															
DEL NORTE	31	164	228	155	232	101	139	223	218	183	58	164	297	37	182														
DELTA	209	120	267	199	279	170	208	293	243	253	237	157	192	175	251	183													
DENVER	212	162	30	81	22	117	115	30	34	70	240	377	208	251	115	213	261												
DOVE CREEK	230	282	417	344	420	289	327	412	395	372	257	35	317	205	370	199	142	402											
DURANGO	149	249	347	274	350	219	257	342	336	302	177	45	321	124	300	118	129	332	81										
EAGLE	192	72	134	66	146	92	163	155	110	172	220	290	125	230	164	193	133	128	285	262									
ESTES PARK	280	204	36	123	59	185	183	98	63	138	308	445	182	318	183	281	296	71	450	399	165								
FAIRPLAY	132	100	96	22	99	87	75	98	85	64	180	297	168	171	76	133	202	81	322	252	88	150							
FORT COLLINS	274	223	46	141	53	179	177	92	82	132	302	439	202	313	177	275	322	55	464	394	189	42	143						
FORT MORGAN	290	238	87	157	61	195	193	108	111	148	318	455	285	328	193	291	337	81	479	409	204	102	158	87					
GEORGETOWN	189	116	52	45	53	92	132	73	28	112	217	354	153	228	133	190	216	45	368	309	83	88	57	106	122				
GLENWOOD SP	204	41	165	97	177	104	187	186	141	198	232	258	116	242	190	205	100	150	254	231	31	196	119	220	236	114			
GOLDEN	208	148	20	67	31	113	127	43	21	82	236	372	195	246	127	209	248	15	397	327	115	56	78	74	90	32	146		
GRAND JUNCTION	249	130	254	198	265	194	248	275	230	287	278	197	152	215	279	233	40	248	165	169	120	285	208	308	324	202	89	234	
GREELEY	264	212	54	131	33	169	166	82	86	122	292	426	233	302	167	285	315	54	453	383	178	50	132	30	51	96	209	64	286
GUNNISON	122	146	211	138	214	83	121	206	201	196	150	201	196	150	201	218	107	87	196	206	173	176	295	116	256	273	173	162	191
HOT SULPHUR SP	223	150	108	89	115	136	166	125	80	164	251	386	111	262	167	224	227	97	378	343	94	71	91	114	174	60	125	84	213
IDAHO SPRINGS	201	128	40	41	51	104	145	61	16	101	229	366	175	240	146	202	227	34	379	321	94	78	89	94	110	12	126	20	214
KIOWA	226	220	80	143	72	157	108	23	85	63	254	410	259	284	108	246	316	63	435	365	178	121	102	115	127	96	209	67	296
LA JUNTA	147	247	202	198	184	102	145	207	105	175	341	345	215	150	177	310	175	376	296	265	243	177	237	181	217	290	189	350	
LAKE CITY	120	201	266	193	269	138	176	261	256	221	148	222	314	52	219	90	125	251	242	178	220	331	320	326	228	198	246	163	213
LAS ANIMAS	166	266	221	218	213	203	121	164	226	124	194	360	364	230	169	198	329	194	395	315	284	262	196	258	200	236	309	208	349
LEADVILLE	134	59	109	41	120	34	117	130	85	129	162	296	162	172	121	135	179	103	324	254	58	145	83	164	179	57	89	88	178
LIMON	228	230	111	168	103	168	118	67	122	73	256	421	296	294	118	257	325	88	445	375	215	153	157	147	83	133	246	101	336
LITTLETON	209	168	37	99	29	114	106	22	42	61	236	373	216	247	106	209	269	11	398	328	136	77	73	88	53	167	24	255	
LONGMONT	247	196	15	115	26	152	65	51	105	275	412	215	286	150	248	295	38	437	367	162	23	116	31	79	79	193	47	282	
LOVELAND	261	210	34	129	41	167	165	80	69	120	289	427	212	300	165	263	310	53	451	381	177	30	130	12	72	94	208	62	296
MEEKER	272	109	233	165	244	172	255	254	209	266	300	300	48	310	258	273	143	227	269	273	99	231	187	251	303	182	68	214	104
MONTE VISTA	17	162	227	154	230	99	137	220	217	180	45	177	296	51	181	14	192	212	213	132	192	281	132	274	289	189	203	207	231
MONTROSE	187	141	276	203	280	146	186	271	265	231	215	138	254	230	172	21	26	278	124	108	154	318	181	323	339	238	123	256	81
OURAY	221	177	312	239	315	184	222	307	300	287	249	118	249	196	265	191	57	297	125	72	190	355	217	389	374	274	159	290	97
PAGOSA SPRINGS	89	222	287	214	291	159	197	282	277	242	117	105	356	64	241	59	189	272	140	60	252	341	192	334	350	259	264	267	239
PUEBLO	122	184	139	136	131	121	39	82	144	42	150	316	282	190	87	152	247	112	351	271	202	281	112	221	154	227	126	287	
SAGUACHE	52	127	192	118	195	64	102	187	181	147	80	201	261	74	145	37	157	176	236	155	156	246	97	230	254	154	168	172	196
SALIDA	83	88	153	80	157	28	57	142	143	102	111	248	222	121	107	84	153	136	272	202	118	207	58	200	216	115	130	133	193
SAN LUIS	41	204	250	195	242	141	151	193	255	153	40	236	338	109	190	72	250	223	271	190	233	271	146	285	305	231	245	237	290
SILVERTON	198	200	335	262	338	207	245	330	323	290	228	94	272	173	289	168	80	320	130	49	213	378	240	382	398	297	182	315	120
STEAMBOAT SP	254	155	177	104	184	154	200	193	148	209	282	373	42	293	201	255	216	165	359	345	83	140	126	160	243	111	114	153	194
STERLING	335	281	132	208	104	240	227	153	156	162	363	499	304	373	227	336	362	125	524	454	249	147	203	102	45	167	290	125	379
TELLURIDE	253	207	342	269	348	214	252	337	330	297	291	77	279	220	296	237	87	327	107	118	220	385	247	389	404	304	189	322	127
TRINIDAD	109	242	224	221	216	179	125	167	229	127	137	304	367	177	172	140	304	197	339	259	272	265	199	259	252	240	283	211	336
VAIL	172	102	104	36	116	92	133	125	82	142	190	320	131	210	164	173	163	98	315	292	30	160	58	159	174	53	61	85	150
WALDEN	267	194	154	113	155	170	210	164	125	204	295	432	101	306	211	268	258	143	410	387	125	117	135	101	183	106	156	130	245
WALSENBURG	73	205	187	184	179	142	88	130	192	90	100	267	330	141	135	103	267	160	302	222	235	228	162	222	238	203	247	174	307
WESTCLIFFE	137	144	173	127	165	81	46	116	178	165	301	273	174	121	137	206	148	325	255	174	214	208	224	163	185	160	248		

Colorado Fishing Information

The Colorado Division of Wildlife provides information on fishing conditions around the state through a telephone system. Information is updated every week, year-round.

General fishing conditions 303-291-7533
All regions 291-7534
Metro Denver 291-7535
Northeast 291-7536
Northwest 291-7537
Southeast 291-7538
Southwest 291-7539

Mileage chart (columns read across the diagonal labels: GREELEY, GUNNISON, HOT SULPHUR SPRINGS, IDAHO SPRINGS, KIOWA, LA JUNTA, LAKE CITY, LAS ANIMAS, LEADVILLE, LIMON, LITTLETON, LONGMONT, LOVELAND, MEEKER, MONTE VISTA, MONTROSE, OURAY, PAGOSA SPRINGS, PUEBLO, SAGUACHE, SALIDA, SAN LUIS, SILVERTON, STEAMBOAT SPRINGS, STERLING, TELLURIDE, TRINIDAD, VAIL, WALDEN, WALSENBURG):

City	Distances
GUNNISON	247
HOT SULPHUR SP	122 207
IDAHO SPRINGS	84 185 62
KIOWA	105 229 146 84
LA JUNTA	227 224 268 206 142
LAKE CITY	302 55 262 240 284 267
LAS ANIMAS	246 243 286 225 160 19 286
LEADVILLE	153 118 91 69 153 220 173 239
LIMON	134 239 183 121 44 98 294 117 190
LITTLETON	62 192 103 41 45 196 247 185 110 88
LONGMONT	35 231 104 67 88 210 286 229 137 120 46 18
LOVELAND	21 245 101 82 100 225 300 244 151 135 60 18
MEEKER	280 230 159 193 277 357 266 376 138 314 255 263 260
MONTE VISTA	263 105 223 201 243 164 103 183 134 245 206 247 261 271
MONTROSE	312 65 248 250 294 289 101 306 183 305 257 298 311 165 170
OURAY	348 101 283 266 330 324 137 343 219 340 293 332 346 200 204 36
PAGOSA SPRINGS	323 165 283 261 305 236 117 255 194 316 268 307 322 332 72 188 132
PUEBLO	164 161 205 143 105 64 216 83 155 114 103 147 162 294 139 226 262 211
SAGUACHE	228 70 188 166 210 199 125 218 98 220 173 212 226 236 35 135 171 96 141
SALIDA	189 66 149 127 165 160 121 179 60 176 134 173 188 198 82 132 187 143 97 47
SAN LUIS	275 163 265 254 216 137 161 156 175 218 215 256 273 313 58 229 263 131 112 93 124
SILVERTON	371 124 307 308 353 345 160 364 242 364 316 355 370 224 181 56 23 109 285 194 191 238
STEAMBOAT SP	190 238 69 133 217 303 293 322 120 254 174 173 170 91 254 237 272 314 240 219 180 295 296
STERLING	96 318 217 155 152 200 373 225 224 105 133 123 117 348 334 383 419 394 221 299 260 325 442 292
TELLURIDE	378 131 314 316 380 355 167 374 249 371 323 362 377 230 236 66 50 178 292 201 198 295 74 335 449
TRINIDAD	249 217 290 226 190 81 230 100 214 166 189 232 247 351 126 263 318 199 86 162 154 100 308 325 277 349
VAIL	148 156 104 64 148 258 221 277 38 185 106 132 147 129 172 184 220 232 178 136 98 213 243 96 219 250 310
WALDEN	131 251 61 110 188 309 306 328 135 230 151 132 114 149 267 279 315 327 249 232 193 308 338 58 204 345 334 140
WALSENBURG	212 181 253 191 153 74 193 93 177 156 152 195 210 314 90 246 281 162 49 125 117 63 271 289 263 312 37 215 296
WESTCLIFFE	198 119 197 127 193 116 174 137 116 193 135 185 220 196 56 100 56 124 243 231 258 250 98 154 241 61

Colorado Fishing Regulations————————

Colorado Division of Wildlife, 6060 Broadway, Denver, CO 80216

These regulations have been edited for trout and fly fishing. For complete information, copies of *Colorado Fishing Season Information* are available free of charge from the Colorado Division of Wildlife and fishing supply stores.

License Fees
Licenses are required of everyone 15 years of age and older.

Resident license	$11.00
(6 months for residency)	
2-day license	7.00
1-day stamp	3.00
(required in addition to a short-term license)	
Nonresident license	35.00
10-day license	18.00
2-day license	7.00
1-day stamp	3.00
(required in addition to a short-term license)	

Military and handicapped licenses . . . . free (under certain circumstances, check with Division of Wildlife for details)

Creel limits
Limits are the maximum total for catch and possession, regardless of how many are consumed.

	Daily Limit	Possession Limit
Brook trout (8" or less)	10	10
Lake trout	2	2
All other trout	8	8

(possession of greenback cutthroat trout is illegal)

Except where otherwise noted, fishing is permitted 24 hours a day, year-round.

Area 1: Arkansas River and tributaries
- Season exceptions: Some lakes and reservoirs have limited seasons because of migratory waterfowl. *No fishing year-round*: Clear Creek Reservoir State Wildlife Area from dam, spillway, outlet structures and downstream to U.S. Highway 24.
- Artificial flies or lures only: Arkansas River from Stockyard Bridge

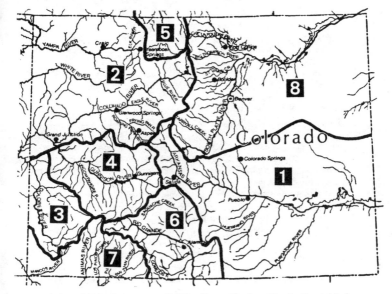

below Salida downstream 7 1/2 miles to Badger Creek; Crystal Lake; Daigre Lake; Lake Dorothey State Wildlife Area; North Lake State Wildlife Area; Rosemont Reservoir; Wahotoya Lake.

- Trout limit exceptions: Arkansas River from Stockyard Bridge below Salida downstream 7 1/2 miles to Badger Creek, 2 trout (16″ or longer); Twin Lakes, 1 lake (20″ or longer); Wahotoya Lake, 2 trout (16″ or longer).
- Wild Trout Water: Arkansas River below Texas Creek downstream to 1 1/2 miles above Parkdale and from Gas Creek downstream to Four Mile Creek.
- Gold Medal Water: Arkansas River below Salida downstream to Fern Leaf Gulch.

Area 2: Colorado River and tributaries
- Season exceptions: *No fishing October 1—December 31* on North Fork of Colorado River from Shadow Mountain Dam Spillway to Twin Creek Inlet of Lake Granby and Granby Reservoir in Columbine Bay to Twin Creek Inlet. *No fishing October 1—January 31* on Blue River from southern boundary of Breckenridge downstream to Dillon Reservoir and Swan River from Blue River upstream 3 miles. *No fishing October 1—February 28* on Walker Lake State Wildlife Area. *No fishing January 1— July 31* on Clinton Creek and Reservoir within 50 yards of Clinton

Reservoir inlet; Clinton Creek upstream for 1/4 mile and Freeman Reservoir within 50 yards of inlet and upstream 1/4 mile; Trappers Lake in the outlet and downstream 1/4 mile and within 100 yeards of each inlet and outlet stream. *No fishing 9:00 PM to 7:00 AM* in West Lake State Wildlife Area. *No fishing year-round*: White River from Taylor Draw Reservoir Dam to 400 yards downstream as posted; Trappers Lake in all inlets and upstream for 1/2 mile.

■ Trout limit exceptions: Blue River from southern edge of Breckenridge downstream to Colorado River (except for Dillon and Green Mountain Reservoirs), 2 trout, (16″ or longer); Bull Creek Reservoir #1 and #2 and connecting channels, 2 trout, (16″ or longer); Clinton Creek and Reservoir, 2 trout, (16″ or longer); Colorado River from lower boundary of Pioneer Park to Troublesome Creek, 2 trout, (16″ or longer); Dillon Reservoir, 8 trout and salmon combined; Eagle River from Gore Creek downstream to Highway 6 bridge, 2 trout; Fraser River from Meadow Creek downstream to Colorado River, 2 trout; Frying Pan River from lower boundary of U.S. Forest Service lands to Roaring Fork, 2 trout, (16″ or longer); Gore Creek from Red Sandstone Creek downstream to Eagle River, 2 trout, (16″ or longer); Granby Reservoir, 1 lake trout, (20″ or longer); Green Mountain Reservoir, 1 lake trout (20″ or longer); Griffith Reservoir, 2 trout, (16″ or longer); Hollenbeck Reservoir, 2 trout; Juniata Reservoir, 2 trout; Roaring Fork River from Upper Woody Creek Bridge to Colorado River, 2 trout, (16″ or longer); Silver Lake, 2 game fish, (16″ or longer); Swan River, 2 rainbow or brown trout, (16″ or longer); Trappers Lake, trout 11″—16″ must be released; Williams Fork Reservoir, 1 lake trout, (20″ or longer); Yampa River from Catamount Dam downstream to Elk River, 2 trout.

■ Artificial flies and lures only: Allen Basin Reservoir; Arapaho Creek from Monarch Lake downstream to County Highway Bridge; Blue River from Green Mountain Dam downstream to Colorado River; Bobtail Creek from headwaters downstream to Denver Water Board Diversion; Bull Creek Reservoirs #1 and #2 and connecting channels; Cabin Creek (catch-and-release only); Clinton Creek and Reservoir; Colorado River from lower boundary of Pioneer Park to Troublesome Creek; Corral Creek (catch-and-release only); Cunningham Creek (catch-and-release only); Fawn Creek (catch-and-release only); Frying Pan River from Ruedi Dam downstream to lower boundary of U.S. Forest Service lands (catch-and-release only) and below Forest Service lands to Roaring Fork; Gore Creek from Red Sandstone Creek downstream to Eagle River; Griffith Reservoir; Hat Creek(catch-and-release only); Hollenbeck Reservoir; Juniata Reservoir; Little Vasquez Creek from headwaters downstream to Denver Water Board Diversion (catch-and-release only); East Meadow Creek (catch-and-release only); Mitchell Creek from headwaters downstream to Glenwood Springs Fish Hatchery (catch-and- release only); Pearl Lake; Roaring Fork River from Hallum Lake downstream to Upper Woody Creek Bridge (catch-and-release only) and from bridge downstream to Colorado River; Silver Lake; Steelman Creek (catch-and-release only); North Fork of Swan Creek (catch-and-release only); Swan River; Trappers Lake.

- Wild Trout Water: Blue River from Green Mountain Dam downstream to Colorado River; Colorado River from upper end of Gore Canyon downstream to State Bridge; Fraser River from 1 mile below Tabernash downstream to 1 mile above Granby; Roaring Fork River from Hallum Lake downstream to Upper Woody Creek Bridge; Trappers Lake.
- Gold Medal Water: Blue River from Green Mountain Dam downstream to Colorado River; Colorado River from Fraser River downstream to Troublesome Creek; Frying Pan River from Ruedi Dam downstream to Roaring Fork; Gore Creek; Roaring Fork River from Crystal River downstream to Colorado River.

Area 3: Dolores River and tributaries
- Artificial flies and lures only: Bear Creek from headwaters downstream to Dolores River; Dolores River from McPhee Dam downstream to Bradfield Bridge (catch-and-release only); Navajo Lake; West Fork of Dolores River from Navajo Lake downstream to Burro Bridge; Woods Lake State Wildlife Area.

Area 4: Gunnison River and tributaries
- Season exceptions: *No fishing January 1—June 30* on Blue Mesa Reservoir from high water line at Coal Creek Inlet upstream 1 mile. *No fishing year-round*: Gunnison River from Crystal Dam downstream for 200 yards, from Blue Mesa Dam downstream for 200 yards, from Morrow Point Dam downstream for 130 yards.
- Trout limit exceptions: Blue Mesa Reservoir, 1 lake trout (20″ or longer); East River from upstream boundary of Roaring Judy Fish Hatchery downstream to Taylor River, 8 trout (12″ or less); Gunnison River from upstream boundary of Black Canyon National Monument to North Fork of Gunnison, 4 trout (only 1 longer than 16″, must release all other trout longer than 16″, release all trout between 12″-16″; San Cristobal Lake, 1 lake trout (20″ or longer); Taylor Reservoir, 1 lake trout, 20″ or longer.
- Artificial flies and lures only: Anthracite Creek from Erickson Springs Campground bridge to North and Middle Forks; Archuleta Creek on Coleman Ranches (catch-and-release only); Cochetopa Creek on Coleman Ranches (catch- and-release only); East River from upstream property boundary of Roaring Judy Fish Hatchery downstream to Taylor River; Lake Fork of Gunnison from Lake San Cristobal inlet upstream to first bridge crossing; Gunnison River from upstream boundary of Black Canyon National Monument to North Fork of Gunnison; Henson

Creek from North Henson Creek downstream to Fanny Fern Mine road; Los Pinos Creek on Coleman Ranches (catch-and-release only); Wild Trout Water: East River from bridge at Roaring Judy Fish Hatchery downstream to Taylor River; Gunnison River from upstream boundary of Black Canyon National Monument to North Fork of Gunnison; Los Pinos Creek within Cochetopa State Wildlife Area.

- Gold Medal Water: Gunnison River from upstream boundary of Black Canyon National Monument to North Fork of Gunnison.

Area 5: North Platte River and tributaries

- Season exceptions: *No fishing year-round* on Canadian River within Trick State Wildlife Area and Michigan River within Trick State Wildlife Area.
- Trout limit exceptions: North Delaney Butte Lake, release all brown trout between 14″-18″; Laramie River within Hohnholz State Wildlife Area, 2 trout; North Platte River from southern boundary of Routt National Forest downstream to state line, 2 trout.
- Artificial flies and lures only: Agnes Lake; Clear Lake; Grizzly Creeks on the Peterson State Wildlife Area; Hohnholz Lake #3; Illinois River on the MacNaughton State Wildlife Area; Kelly Lake; Laramie River within the Hohnholz State Wildlife Area; Michigan River on the Brownlee, MacNaughton and Murphy State Wildlife Areas; North and East Delaney Buttes Lakes; North Fork Michigan Reservoir; North Platte River from southern boundary of Routt National Forest downstream to state line and on the Brownlee, Manville, Peterson, Trick, Verner, and Wilford State Wildlife Areas; North Fork of North Platte River in Richards State Wildlife Area; Raspberry Creek on Irvin State Wildflife Area; Roaring Fork Creek on Irvine and Odd Fellows State Wildlife Area; Ruby Jewel Lake.
- Wild Trout Water: North Platte River from southern boundary of Routt National Forest downstream to state line.
- Gold Medal Water: North Delaney Butte Lake; North Platte River from southern boundary of Routt National Forest downstream to state line.

Area 6: Rio Grande and tributaries

- Season exceptions: *No fishing March 15—June 30* on BLM Ponds in Blanca Wildlife Habitat Area. *No fishing March 15—July 15* on San Luis Lakes State Wildlife Area north of buoy line and adjacent east-west fence line as posted. *No fishing year-round*: Jim Creek; Torsido Creek.
- Trout limit exceptions: Rio Grande from Coller Bridge downstream to west fence of Masonic Park, 2 trout (16″ or longer).
- Artificial flies and lures only: Bear Creek from headwaters downstream to Conejos River; Conejos River on property of Rainbow Lodge, Hamilton Ranch, H.E.B.O. Corporation, and Mead from Menkhaven down-

stream to Aspen Glade Campground (fly fishing only); Forbes Park Lake (catch-and-release only); Kerr Lake; Lake Fork of Conejos River from headwaters (including Big Lake) downstream to Rock Lake, including Rock Lake and outlet (catch-and-release only); Rio Grande from Coller Bridge downstream to west fence of Masonic Park; San Francisco Creek (Middle and West Forks) on U.S. Forest Service lands including West San Francisco Lake (catch- and-release only); Sheep Creek from head-water downstream to Conejos River.

- Wild Trout Water: Cascade Creek; Conejos River from Menkhaven Ranch downstream to Aspen Glade Campground; Lake Fork of Conejos River from headwaters downstream to natural dam at Rock Lake outlet; Osier Creek.
- Gold Medal Water: Rio Grande from upper boundary of Coller State Wildlife Area downstream to Farmers Union Canal.

Area 7: San Juan River and tributaries.
- Trout limit exceptions: Emerald Lakes, 8 trout (12″ or less).
- Artificial flies and lures only: Emerald Lakes; Los Pinos River from headwaters to Weminuche Wilderness Area boundary; Piedra River from first fork downstream to Lower Piedra Campground; Vallecito Creek from headwaters to Weminuche Wilderness Area boundary.
- Wild Trout Water: Emerald Lakes.

Area 8: South Platte River and tributaries.
- Season exceptions: *No fishing January 1—July 31* on Joe Wright Creek and Reservoir from bridge downstream to, and including the reservoir. *No fishing April 15—May 31* on South Platte River from City of Aurora property line downstream to Spinney Mt. Reservoir inlet. *No fishing September 1—December 1* on South Platte River from Spinney Mt. Dam downstream about 1 mile. *No fishing November 1—April 30* on Cheesman Reservoir and inlets. *No fishing 9:00 PM—4:00 AM* on Gross Reservoir. *No fishing May 1—July 15* on Long Lake. *No fishing November 1—April 30* in Parvin State Wildlife Area. *No fishing January 1—July 31* on Zimmerman Lake. *No fishing year-round*: Bard Creek from headwaters downstream to West Fork of Clear Creek; Black Hollow Creek from headwaters downstream to Poudre River; Bruno Gulch from headwaters downstream to Geneva Creek; Clear Creek Holding Ponds; Como Creek from headwaters downstream to North Boulder Creek; Cornelius Creek from headwaters downstream to Sheep Creek, as posted; George Creek from headwaters downstream to Cornelius Creek; Hourglass Creek from headwaters downstream to Hourglass Reservoir; Lawn Lake (Rocky Mt. National Park); Lone Tree Reservoir State Wildlife Area in outlet canal, as posted; May Creek from headwaters downstream to Poudre River; Parvin Lake State Wildlife Area in inlet

stream from lake upstream to Red Feather Lake Road, as posted; Roaring River in Rocky Mt. National Park; Sheep Creek (East and West Forks) from headwaters downstream to Poudre River; South Fork of Poudre River from Rocky Mt. National Park boundary downstream 1 mile; Valmont Reservoir, as posted; Williams Gulch from headwaters downstream to Poudre River; Zinn Ranch Ponds and connecting streams upstream to headwaters of Jackson Creek.

■ Trout limit exceptions: Big Thompson River from Noel's Draw bridge downstream to Waltonia bridge, 2 trout (16″ or longer); Cheesman Reservoir and inlets, 2 trout (16″ or longer); Joe Wright Creek and Reservoir from bridge downstream to, and including reservoir, 2 trout (16″ or longer); Lake Isabelle, 2 trout (12″ or longer); Long Lake, 2 trout (12″ or longer); Middle Fork of South Platte River from U.S. Highway 285 bridge downstream (except Antero Reservoir) to Middle Fork of South Platte River (including Knight-Imler State Wildlife Area), 8 trout (no more than 2 16″ or longer); North St. Vrain Creek from Horse Creek downstream to Button Rock Resevoir inlet, 2 trout; Poudre River from Poudre Valley Canal dam upstream to Monroe Gravity Canal dam, from Grandpa's Bridge upstream to west boundary of Hombre Ranch, from Black Hollow Creek upstream to Poudre Fish Rearing Unit dam, 2 trout (16″ or longer); Quincy Reservoir, 2 trout (16″ or longer); South St. Vrain Creek from headwaters downstream to Brainard Lake Road, 2 trout (12″ or longer); South Platte River from confluence of South and Middle Forks (except Spinney Mt. Reservoir) downstream to Elevenmile Reservoir inlet, 8 trout (no more than 2 16″ or longer); South Platte River from lower boundary of Wigwam Club to Scraggy View Campground, 2 trout (16″ or longer); South Platte River from Scraggy View Picnic Ground downstream to Strontia Springs, 2 trout; South Platte River from Strontia Springs Dam downstream to 300 yeards upstream from Denver Water Board's diversion structure, 2 trout (16″ or longer); Spinney Mt. Reservoir, 4 trout.

■ Artificial flies and lures only: Big Thompson River from Noel's Draw bridge downstream to Waltonia bridge; Cheesman Reservoir including South Platte River inlet and Goose Creek inlet from Denver Water Board property boundary to reservoir; Chicago Creek from Idaho Springs Reservoir to West Chicago Creek; Joe Wright Creek and Reservoir from bridge downstream to, and including, the reservoir; Lake Isabelle; Long Draw Creek and Reservoir; Long Lake; North St. Vrain Creek from Horse Creek downstream to Button Rock Reservoir inlet; Parvin Lake State Wildlife Area; Poudre River from Poudre Valley Canal dam upstream to Monroe Gravity Canal dam, from Grandpa's Bridge upstream to west boundary of Hombre Ranch, from Black Hollow Creek upstream to Poudre Fish Rearing Unit dam, from Rocky Mountain National Park boundary upstream to Long Draw Creek; Prospect Park Lakes (Bass

Lake and West Prospect Lake); Quincy Reservoir; Sawhill Ponds (except ponds #1 and #1A); South St. Vrain Creek from headwaters downstream to Brainard Lake Road; Middle Fork of South Platte River from 3/4 mile above State Highway 9 bridge downstream to South Fork of South Platte River (including Tomahawk State Wildlife Area); South Fork of South Platte River from U.S. Highway 285 bridge downstream (except Antero Reservoir) to Middle Fork (including Knight-Imler State Wildlife Area); South Platte River from confluence of South and Middle Forks downstream (except for Spinney Mt. Reservoir) to Elevenmile Reservoir inlet, from Cheesman Dam downstream to Upper Wigwam property line, from lower boundary of Wigwam Club to Scraggy View Campground, from Strontia Springs Dam downstream to 300 yards upstream from Denver Water Board's diversion structure; South Boulder Creek from 1/2 mile below Gross Reservoir Dam downstream to South Boulder Road; Tarryall Creek from County Road 77 downstream to Ute Creek Trail Bridge; Trout Creek from 1 1/4 miles within Tomahawk State Wildlife Area downstream to Middle Fork of South Platte; Ward Pond; Watson Lake State Wildlife Area, as posted; Zimmerman Lake.

■ Catch-and-release only: Fern Lake and Creek (Rocky Mt. National Park); Ouzel Lake and Creek (Rocky Mt. National Park); South Platte River from Cheesman Dam downstream to Upper Wigwam property line.

■ Wild Trout Water: Poudre River from Poudre Valley Canal dam upstream to Monroe Gravity Canal dam, from Grandpa's Bridge upstream to west boundary of Hombre Ranch, from Black Hollow Creek upstream to Poudre Fish Rearing Unit dam, from Rocky Mountain National Park boundary upstream to Long Draw Creek; North St. Vrain Creek from Horse Creek downstream to Button Rock Reservoir; Middle Fork of South Platte River within Tomahawk State Wildlife area; South Platte River from Beaver Creek downstream to Cheesman Reservoir; Tarryall Creek from Pike National Forest boundary downstream to South Platte River.

■ Gold Medal Water: Middle Fork of South Platte River from 3/4 mile above State Highway 9 bridge to lower boundary of Tomakawk State Wildlife Area; South Platte River from Cheesman Dam downstream to North Fork.

Rocky Mountain National Park

■ A valid Colorado fishing license is required within the boundaries of the park, and all state fishing regulations apply, with the following exceptions: Trout limit exception is 8 trout, with at least 6 being brook trout, and the others at least 10″ or longer. An additional limit of 10 brook trout (under 8″) is allowed. ■ Possession of greenback cutthroat trout is prohibited. ■ Fishing is permitted only with artificial flies or lures with one (single, double, or treble) hook with a common shank. ■ Children

12 years of age and under may possess and use worms or preserved fish eggs in open park waters except for catch-and-release waters. ■ Catch-and-release waters require artificial flies or lures having one barbless hook. ■ Possession or use for fishing purposes of natural bait, including worms, insects, fish eggs, live or dead minnows, or part thereof, is prohibited with the exception noted.

- No fishing year-round in outlet waters and pools of Lake Nanita from lakeshore to a point 100 yards downstream.
- No fishing or restricted fishing in special native trout waters (posted in areas and published in newspapers when changed): West Creek, Ouzel Lake and Ouzel Creek, Fern Lake and Fern Creek drainage, Timber Lake and Timber Creek, Lawn Lake, Roaring River, North Fork of the Big Thompson River above Lost Falls.
- Catch-and-release only: Hidden Valley Creek from beaver ponds at Hidden Valley to Fall River, as posted; Big Thompson River in Forest Canyon above Spruce Creek; Fay Lake drainage, including Caddis Lake.

Wyoming Fishing Regulations

Wyoming Game and Fish Department, Cheyenne, WY 82002

These regulations have been edited for trout and fly fishing. For complete information, copies of *Wyoming Fishing Regulations* are available free of charge from the Wyoming Game and Fish Department and fishing supply stores.

License Fees

Licenses are required of everyone 14 years of age and older.

Resident license .... $	7.50
(12 months for residency)	
Nonresident	35.00
Tourist 1-day	5.00
10-day license	20.00
Youth (14-19)	3.00
Nonresident youth (10-day)	10.00
Military license	10.00
Conservation stamp	5.00
(required in addition to all licenses except Tourist 1-day)	

Creel limits
(Daily bag and possession limit)

> Brook trout 10
> (in addition to general trout limit)
> All other trout 6
> (in any combination, only one fish longer than 20″)

There are five fishing areas defined by specific boundaries within the state. Except where otherwise noted, fishing is permitted from 4:00 AM to 10:00 PM (MST or MDT)

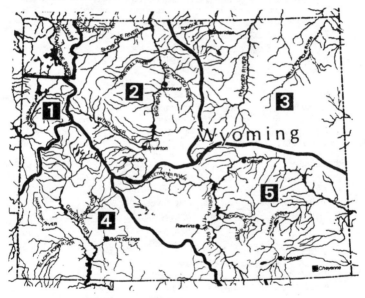

Area 1: Snake River, Salt River, Greys River, Hoback River, Gros Ventre River, Buffalo Fork River, and all drainages west of the Teton Range. For more information: Area Fisheries Supervisor, Box 67, Jackson, WY 83001

- Season dates: Fishing is permitted year-round in Palisades Reservoir, Salt River Drainage below the Upper Narrows Bridge (Wyoming Highway 238), Jenny Lake, Leigh Lake, Two Ocean Lake, Grassy Lake Reservoir, Phelps Lake, Boyles Hill Ponds, Lower Slide Lake, Elk Park Pond, Flat Creek (between west boundary of Federal Elk Refuge and

U.S. Highway 191 bridge at Sagebrush Motel—age 13 and younger only). *November 1—September 30* on Jackson Lake. *January 1—October 31* on Salt River drainage above the Upper Narrows Bridge (Wyoming Highway 238). *April 1—October 31* on Snake River from Palisades Reservoir to Yellowstone Park boundary and downstream drainage from Snake River Bridge at Hoback Junction, Hoback River, Greys River, all water west of Teton Range. *May 21—October 31* on Snake River Drainage (not including Snake River itself) upstream from the Snake River Bridge (at Hoback Junction) with following exceptions: *August 1—October 31* on Cottonwood Creek, Blacktail Spring Creek and Upper Bar BC Spring Creek (in Grand Teton National Park), Lower Bar BC Spring Creek and Flat Creek (between Old Crawford Bridge and McBride Bridge on Federal Elk Refuge). *No fishing year-round* on Nowlin Creek and Flat Creek drainage (in the Federal Elk Refuge from Old Crawford Bridge downstream to refuge boundary), Lake-of-the-Woods, Snake River from 150 feet below downstream face of Jackson Lake Dam, Swan, Lake, Sawmill Pond, Moose Pond, Hedrick's Pond, Christian Pond, Cottonwood Creek (from the outlet of Jenny Lake downstream to Saddle Horse Concession Bridge in Teton County).

■ Trout limit exceptions: Snake River from 1000 feet below Jackson Lake Dam (gauging station) to highway bridge at Moose, and all tributaries of Snake between these points (within Grand Teton National Park) except for Buffalo Fork River, 4 trout (only 1 longer than 15″, 11-15″ trout must be released immediately); Jackson Lake, Jenny Lake, Leigh Lake, 6 trout (only 1 longer than 24″).

■ Artificial flies only: Flat Creek between Old Crawford Bridge and McBride Bridge (on Federal Elk Refuge).

■ Artificial flies and lures only: Pacific Creek upstream from mouth to boundary of Teton National Forest.

Area 2: Wind River, Big Horn River Canyon, Shoshone River, Clark's Fork and Yellowstone River drainages.
For more information: Area Fisheries Supervisor, 260 Buena Vista, Lander, WY 82520 or 2820 State Hwy. 120, Cody, WY 82414

■ Season dates: *May 1—August 31* on all lakes, streams, and ponds within the drainage of Badwater Creek and Buffalo Creek (within Hot Springs, Fremont, Natrona counties). *June 1—March 31* on Torrey Creek (from Torrey Lake to national forest boundary). *June 1—August 31* on Shoshone Lake, Shoshone Creek. *July 1—March 31* on North Fork of the Shoshone River Drainage (from Gibbs Bridge upstream to Newton Creek, inclusive). *July 15—March 31* on Buffalo Bill Reservoir (west of line connecting mouths of Rattlesnake Creek and Sheep Creek), North Fork Shoshone River (from mouth upstream to Gibbs Bridge). *July 15—December 31* on Torrey Creek Drainage (above Ross Lake), Ross

Lake (south of P.J. Island). *August 1—December 31* on Washakie Creek (above Little Washakie Lake), Washakie Lake within 50 feet of outlet and all inlets, all tributaries to lake. *No fishing year-round* on rise of the Middle Fork of the Popo Agie River (downstream to bridge on Sinks Canyon Road), Lake-of- the-Woods.

■ Trout limit exceptions: Eastside drainages of the Bighorn River (not including Bighorn River proper) between state line and Nowater Creek, 12 trout (only 1 longer than 20″); Clark's Fork drainage (not including Clark's Fork River proper below Dead Indian Creek), 12 trout (only 1 longer than 20″); North Fork Shoshone River Drainage, 6 trout (only 1 cutthroat, only 1 longer than 20″); Yellowstone River Drainage (upstream from Yellowstone National Park boundary), 2 trout (only 1 longer than 20″); Lower Newton Lake, 1 trout (minimum 20″, artificial flies and lures only).

■ Other exceptions: Night fishing permitted year-round on Big Horn Lake, Big Horn River (upstream from Big Horn Lake to Robertson Dam), Ocean Lake, Boysen Reservoir, Wind River (downstream from Boysen Dam to Wind River Indian Reservation); December— February fishing permitted (including night fishing) on Ocean Lake, Pilot Butte Reservoir, Ring Lake, Trail Lake, Torrey Lake, Boysen Reservoir, Big Horn Lake, Big Horn River (upstream from Big Horn Lake to Robertson Dam), Wardell Reservoir.

Area 3: Niobara River, Cheyenne River, Stockage-Beaver Creek, Sand Creek, Belle Fourche River, Little Missouri River, Little Powder River, Powder River, Tongue River and Little Horn River drainages.
For more information: Area Fisheries Supervisor, Box F, Buffalo, WY 82834

■ Season dates: *May 1—August 31* on Burlington Reservoir, Sand Creek Public Fishing Area (U.S. Fish and Wildlife Service property at Ranch A). *June 1—April 30* on Lake DeSmet and Shell Creek to the west of Game and Fish Department markers to marked point above state spawning trap.

■ Trout limit exceptions: Bighorn National Forest, 12 trout (including salmon and grayling, only 1 longer than 20″); Sand Creek, 12 trout (only 1 longer than 20″).

■ Artificial flies and lures only: Sand Creek including Public Fishing Area.

■ Other exceptions: Night fishing is permitted on Belle Fourche River proper, Powder River proper, Keyhole Reservoir, Clear Creek (from Kendrick Dam to mouth); Winter fishing is permitted from December through February on Lake DeSmet and Keyhole Reservoir.

■ Class 1 water: Middle Fork of Powder River from mouth of canyon above Bar C Ranch to Hazelton-33 Mile Road, Sand Creek from mouth of Redwater through state land (including Rienecke lease), Sand Creek on Ranch A, Tongue River from forest service line to fork of North and South Tongue Rivers.

■ Class 2 water: Little Bighorn River from state line to Dayton Gulch, North Tongue River, Tongue River in state public fishing area, Sand Creek on Sank Creek Country Club, South Tongue River, South Piney Creek from forest service line to Cloud Peak Reservoir, Piney Creek from confluence downstream about 8 miles, North Fork Powder River from mouth of canyon to Dullknife Reservoir, Big Goose Creek from VA Hospital intake to fork of East and West Goose Creeks, Clear Creek from 6-Mile Ditch to fork of North and South Clear Creek.

Area 4: Green River, Little Snake River, Bear River and Great Divide Basin drainages.

For more information: Area Fisheries Supervisor, Box 850, Pinedale, WY 82941 or 351 Astle Ave., Green River, WY 82935

■ Season dates: *May 1—November 30* on Burnt Lake and Meadow Lake. *May 10—September 30* on Soda Lake. *July 1—March 31* on Lake Alice and upstream tributaries, Meadow Creek, Meadow Lake (east of Game and Fish Department markers), Dempsey Creek, Trail Creek, Ham's Fork River (upstream to Corral Creek), all sloughs and tributaries to Viva Naughton Reservoir, Camp Creek, Fish Creek, Robinson Creek tributary (to Kemmerer City Reservoir), Boulder Creek (above Boulder Lake), Pole Creek (above Halfmoon Lake). *July 15—September 30* on Kemmerer City Reservoir, Ham's Fork River (upstream from Kemmerer City Reservoir to Viva Naughton Dam). *July 16—May 31* on North Piney Lake and upstream tributaries. *August 1—October 31* on Surprise Creek drainage and Surprise Lake. *November 1—October 14* on Green River (from Fontenelle Dam downstream to gauge at Weeping Rocks Campground). *No fishing year-round* on Viva Naughton Dam on upstream side (no fishing from dam), Rock Creek, Flume Creek (below Fontenelle Reservoir), Kendall Warm Springs, Kendall Warm Springs Creek, North Fork of the Little Snake drainage (above West Branch Creek).

■ Trout limit exceptions: Green River Lakes, 6 trout (including salmon and grayling, only 1 longer than 20″, lake trout 16-26″ must be released immediately); Halfmoon Lake, 6 trout (including salmon and grayling, only 1 longer than 20″, only 2 lake trout, lake trout less than 18″ must be released immediately); Green River (from Kendall Warm Springs downstream to Bridger-Teton National Forest), 2 trout (including salmon and grayling, all trout 10-20″ must be released immediately, brook trout limit does not apply, artificial flies and lures only); cutthroat trout 10″ or less must be released immediately (artificial flies and lures only): Beaver Creek drainage, Dry Piney Creek drainage, Fish Creek drainage, Hobble Creek drainage (including Lake Alice), North Cottonwood Creek

drainage and Maki Creek, North Horse Creek and Lead Creek drainages (in Bridger-Teton National Forest), North Piney Creek drainage and North Piney Lake, Smiths Fork drainage (including Porcupine Creek), South Cottonwood Creek drainage (not including Soda Lake ponds), South Horse Creek drainage, Thomas Fork drainage including Raymond Creek (from state line upstream); no extra brook trout permitted in Black's Fork drainage.
- Other exceptions: Night fishing is permitted on Flaming Gorge Reservoir. Flaming Gorge Reservoir regulations: No license required if under 14 years old (only 1/2 daily adult limit allowed); Other state licenses required on portions of reservoir outside of Wyoming; Wyoming license with Utah reciprocal fishing stamp is valid in Utah portions of reservoir (and Utah license with Wyoming reciprocal fishing stamp is valid in Wyoming portion of reservoir); Trout limit is 8 (only 1 trout longer than 20", no more than 2 lake trout); fishing permitted 24 hours daily.

Area 5: North Platte River, Sweetwater River, South Platte River and all drainages.   For more information: Area Fisheries Supervisor, 528 S. Adams, Laramie, WY 82070 or 2800 Pheasant Dr., Casper, WY 82604
- Season dates: *January 16—October 31* on North Springer Reservoir. *January 2—April 30 and May 15—September 30* on Table Mountain Reservoirs. *May 1—October 31* on Alsop Lake. *June 1—October 31* on Rock Creek Reservoir.
- Trout limit exceptions: Alcova Reservoir, 12 trout (including salmon and grayling, only 1 longer than 20"); North Platte River (from Saratoga Inn Bridge upstream to state line), 6 trout (including salmon and grayling, only 1 longer than 16", all trout 10-16" must be released immediately, artificial flies and lures only).
- Other exceptions: Night fishing is permitted on Wheatland Reservoir #1, Joe Johnson Reservoir, Rock Lake, Grayrocks Reservoir and Festo Lake, Hawk Springs Reservoir and Packers Lake, North Platte River and mainstream reservoirs (from Interstate 80 to state line); Winter fishing permitted from December through February on Guernsey Reservoir, Glendo Reservoir, Alcova Reservoir, Pathfinder Reservoir, Seminoe Reservoir, Grayrocks Reservoir.

Grand Teton National Park
- Wyoming state fishing licenses are required within park boundaries and general state fishing regulations apply. ■ No fishing on Snake River for a distance of 150 feet below the downstream face of Jackson Lake Dam, Swan Lake, Sawmill Ponds, Hendrick's Pond, Christian Ponds, and Cottonwood Creek (from the outlet of Jenny Lake downstream to the Saddle Horse Concession Bridge). ■ Boating is controlled; some park waters are closed to boats with motors and rafts. ■ No fishing

from any bridge or boat dock in the Park.
For further information, write to: Grand Teton National Park Headquarters, Moose, WY 83012.

Yellowstone National Park

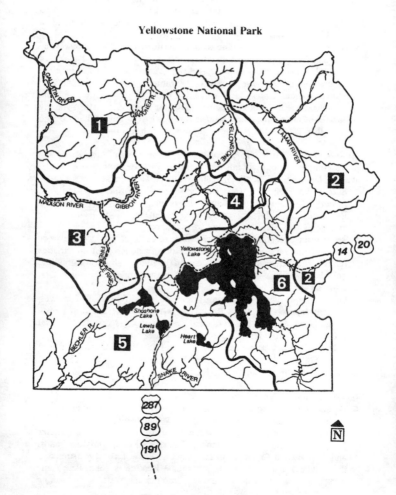

Yellowstone National Park

- Special permit is required (no cost) for all persons 12 years of age and older for fishing within park boundaries; available at all ranger stations within the park. ■ Trout limit is 2 per day or in possession except for listed exceptions. ■ Fishing only with artificial flies on single hook or lures with one single, double, or treble hook (exceptions listed below).
- Possession of fishing bait (including worms, insects, and organic matter) or non-regulation lures is prohibited to anyone with fishing equipment while immediately adjacent to or on park waters.
- Catch-and-release only for grayling.
- Daily fishing permitted from 5:00 AM—10:00 PM local time.

Zone 1: Gallatin River drainage, Grayling Creek, Duck Creek, Cougar Creek, Mol Heron Creek, Reese Creek, Stephen Creek, and Landslide Creek drainages, Gardner River drainage, and Yellowstone River drainage (from north boundary upstream to Inspiration Point, excluding the Lamar River).

- Season: May 28—October 31 on all waters with exceptions.
- Season exception: *no fishing year-round* in Mammoth Water Supply Reservoir; *no fishing* on Gardner River (between Mammoth Hot Springs and North Boundary) as posted from September until end of fishing season.
- Trout limit exceptions: 5 trout per day or in possession (at least 3 must be brook trout) on all waters except catch-and-release and the following waters; 5 trout (at least 3 must be brook or brown trout) on Gallatin River and Grayling Creek and tributaries, Cougar Creek (below Gneiss Creek trail crossing).

Zone 2: Lamar River drainage and Middle Creek drainage east of Sylvan Pass.

- Season: *May 28—October 31* on all waters with exceptions.
- Season exception: *June 15—October 31* on Trout Lake drainage above Soda Butte Creek, including Trout, Buck, and Shrimp Lake.
- Catch-and-release only: Slough Creek and tributaries (including McBride Lake), Lamar River proper from confluence with Yellowstone River upstream to mouth of Cache Creek).

Zone 3: Madison River drainage.

- Season: *May 28—October 31* on all waters with exceptions.
- Season exception: *no fishing year- round* on Old Faithful water supply (Firehole River from Old Faithful water intake to Shoshone Lake trail crossing) and Firehole River (from bridge 1/2 mile east of Old Faithful downstream to bridge at Biscuit Basin and all posted areas in the immediate vicinity of hazardous or fragile thermal features).
- Trout limit exceptions: minimum length limit of 16″ for all trout on the Madison and Firehole Rivers and the lower Gibbon River up to Gibbon Falls.

■ Fly fishing only: Firehole River, Madison River, and Gibbon River extending from mouth to the base of Gibbon Falls.

Zone 4: Yellowstone River drainage from Inspiration Point upstream to 1 mile downstream from Yellowstone Lake outlet.

■ Season: *July 15—October 31* on all waters with exceptions.

■ Season exception: *no fishing year-round* on Yellowstone River and tributaries from Sulphur Caldron downstream to Alum Creek and from Chittenden Bridge downstream to a point directly below Inspiration Point overlook.

■ Catch-and-release only: Yellowstone River proper from 1 mile below Yellowstone Lake outlet downstream to Sulphur Caldron, Yellowstone River proper from Alum Creek downstream to Chittenden Bridge, Cascade Creek drainage near Canyon Village (including Cascade Lake).

Zone 5: all waters on west slope of the Continental Divide.

■ Season: *May 28—October 31.*

■ Catch-and-release only: Lewis River proper below Lewis Falls, Heart Lake and tributaries and the Heart River downstream to Outlet Creek (cutthroat trout only, regular limits apply for lake, brown, and rainbow trout), Pocket Lake, Bechler River and tributaries above Colonnade Falls, Falls River drainage above falls at the 7200 foot contour as posted (including Beula and Herring Lakes).

Zone 6: Yellowstone River drainage (including Yellowstone and Riddle Lakes) from a point 1 mile downstream from Yellowstone Lake outlet upstream to park boundary.

■ Season: *June 15—October 31* for all lakes; *July 15—October 31* for all streams.

■ Season exceptions: no fishing year-round on Yellowstone River and tributaries from Yellowstone Lake outlet to a point 1 mile downstream, Pelican Creek on lower 2 miles, Bridge Bay Lagoon and Marina, Grant Village and Marina and connecting channels with Yellowstone Lake, West Thumb thermal area as posted on shores at southern extreme of Yellowstone Lake to mouth of Little Thumb Creek, Yellowstone Lake shore within 100 yards of the mouth of any stream that is closed to fishing.

■ Catch-and-release only: Pelican Creek and tributaries from 2 miles above mouth to headwaters, Sylvan Lake and inlets and outlet downstream to Clear Creek, Sedge Creek and tributaries above Turbid Lake.

■ Trout limit exceptions: all trout must be under 13".

Wind River Indian Reservation
Fishing within the Reservation is controlled by the tribal council, and a special permit is required. Complete regulations, including camping information, can be obtained from: Fish and Game Office, Tribal Complex, P.O. Box 217, Fort Washakie, WY 82514 (307-332-7207)

License Fees

Resident season	$35.00
(resident of Wyoming or Wind River Indian Reservation)	
Non-resident season	60.00
1-day resident	7.00
1-day non-resident	10.00
7-day resident	25.00
7-day non-resident	35.00
Resident youth	10.00
(season, 14-18 years old)	
Non-resident youth	25.00
Resident senior citizens	15.00
(60 years and older)	
Non-resident senior citizens	35.00
(season)	

Creel limits

Brook trout	no limit on brook trout 10″ or less
Lake trout	2 (only 1 24″ or longer)
all other trout	8 (only 1 20″ or longer)

- Trout limit exceptions: Bull Lake, Dinwoody Lakes, Wind River Canyon, 5 trout (only 1 20″ or longer; 2 lake trout, only 1 24″ or longer).
- Live minnows are permitted as bait with receipt verifying origin of fish (must be from Wind River drainage).
- Season: *year-round fishing* permitted on North Fork of Popo Agie River, Popo Agie River (to Hudson). *April 1—September 30, 4:00 AM— 10:00 PM* on Bull Lake, Bull Lake Creek, Upper and Lower Dinwoody Lakes, Dinwoody Creek (below Lower Dinwoody Lake), Ray Lake, Washakie Reservoir (and upstream), Wind River (including Wind River Canyon beginning at tunnels, downstream to Wedding of the Waters), downstream from confluence of Popo Agie and Little Wind River. *June 1—September 30* on all roadless area lakes and streams, Moccasin Lake. *No fishing year-round* on Dinwoody Creek (above Upper Dinwoody Lake), North Fork of Little Wind River (downstream from Washakie Creek), Yantie Lake, all waters not expressly opened to public fishing.
- No boat fishing except on Bull Lake, Dinwoody Lakes, Ray Lake, Moccasin Lake (no motors).

Index

Acroneuria   29
adams (fly illus.)   20
Aedes   28
alderfly   14, 32
altitude effects   6
altitude sickness   35
Ametropus   22
Amphizoidae   32
Anabolina   27
Animas River   71, 122
ant   15, 32
aquatic beetles   15
Arctopsyche   27
Arkansas River   36, 51, 120,
   132, 133
Baetis   12, 22
barbless hooks   32
beetle   15, 32
Bechler River   144
Belle Fourche River   143
Big Creek   38
Big Goose Creek   38, 144
Big Horn River   37, 142, 143
Big Sandy River   96, 124
Big Thompson River   48, 49,
   120, 138
Bighorn River   82, 123
biting flies   35
black ant   15, 32
black ant (fly illus.)   21
black stonefly (fly illus.)   19
black woolly worm (fly illus.) 19
bloodworm   8, 31
Blue River   36, 56, 121, 133,
   134, 135
body length   34
body parts   5
books   126
Boulder Creek   95, 124, 144
brachycentrus   27
brook trout   3, 4, 5

brown trout   2, 4, 5
Brush Creek   38
Buffalo Fork River   100, 125,
   141, 142
Cache la Poudre River   36, 42,
   49, 50, 120, 137, 138, 143
caddis case   7
caddis case (fly illus.)   18
caddis emerger (fly illus.)   18
caddis nymph (fly illus.)   18
caddis pupa (fly illus.)   18
caddisflies   5, 7, 27, 28
Calineuria   29
Callibaetis   22
Canadian River   136
Cascade Creek   36, 137, 148
catch and release   33
Centroptilum   22, 23
Cheyenne River   143
Chironomidae   31
Cinygmula   23
ciscoe   5
Clark's Fork of Yellowstone
   River   37, 38, 142, 143
Class 1 Water   37
Class 2 Water   38
Clear Creek   38, 87, 123, 137,
   143, 144
Cloeon   23
Cochetopa Creek   37, 61, 121,
   135
Colorado cutthroat   2
Colorado Fishing Information 39
Colorado Fishing Regulations
   132-140
Colorado Fishing Zones Map 133
Colorado map   41
Colorado Mileage Chart   130,
   131
Colorado River   36, 37, 52, 53,
   121, 133, 134, 135

Colorado trout streams 44-73, 120-122
Colorado weather 106-113
Conejos River 37, 73, 121, 136, 137
Copepods 15
craneflies 10
crayfish 5
crustaceans 5, 6, 15
Crystal River 59, 121, 135
cutthroat trout 2, 4, 5
damselflies 5, 13, 32
deerhair beetle (fly illus.) 21
Dicosmoecus 27
Dinwoody Creek 78, 123, 149
dobsonfly 14
Dolores River 69, 122, 135
Douglas Creek 38, 87, 124
dragonfly 13, 32
dragonfly nymph (fly illus.) 19
drakes 11, 12, 13
Drunella 23
dun variant (fly illus.) 20
duns 11, 12, 13
Eagle Creek 38
Eagle River 57, 121, 134
East Fork River 95, 124
East River 37, 60, 61, 135, 136
East Tensleep Creek 38
Elk River 64, 122
elkhair caddis (fly illus.) 19
Empididae 31
Encampment River 38, 88, 124
Epeorus 24
Ephemera 23
Ephemerella 23, 24
Ephoron 24
equipment 16
Federation of Fly Fishers 128
Firehole River 147, 148
first aid 105
fishing conditions 39
flash floods 104
flies 18-21
float tubes 35
floods 6, 104

fly fishing schools 125
fly fishing stores 127
fly line symbols 16
fly line weights 17
fly lines 16, 17
fly rod lengths 16
fly rod weights 16
fly rods 16
fly sizes 17
flying ant 15, 32
Fontenelle Creek 38, 96, 24
food sources 5
Forty Rod Creek 38
Fraser River 37, 54, 121, 134, 135
Frying Pan River 36, 58, 59, 121, 134, 135
Gallatin River 147
Gardner River 74, 123, 147
garter snakes 34
gauging stations 43
giant stonefly 8
giardiasis 35
Gibbon River 147, 148
gnat (fly illus.) 21
Gold Medal Water 36
gold-ribbed hares ear (fly illus.) 18
gold-ribbed hares ear nymph (fly illus.) 18
golden trout 2, 4, 5
Goose Creek 85, 123, 138, 144
Gooseberry Creek 81, 123
Gore Creek 55, 121, 134, 135
Grand Teton National Park 145
grannom 7
grasshopper 15, 32
Green River 37, 38, 93, 124, 144
greenback trout 2
Greybull River 80, 123
Greys River 38, 141, 142
Gros Ventre River 141, 142
Gunnison River 36, 37, 62, 121, 135, 136
Hams Fork River 38, 97, 124, 144

handling 32
hatching charts 22-32
hellgrammite (fly illus.) 19
hellgrammite 14
Hemerobiidae 28
Hemiptera 32
Hendrickson (fly illus.) 20
Henrys Fork River 98, 124
Heptagenia 24
Hexagenia 12, 25
Hoback River 141, 142
hook sizes (illus.) 21
How to Use 1
humpy (fly illus.) 20
Hydropsyche 27
Hypothermia 104
Illinois River 136
imagos 12
insect hatching 6
Insect Hatching Charts 22-32
insects 5, 6
instars 9
Isogenus 29
Isonychia 25
kokanee 5
La Prele Creek 91, 124
lahontan cutthroat 2
Lake Fork of Conejos River 37, 137
lake trout 3, 4, 5
Lamar River 76, 122, 147
Laramie River 37, 45, 92, 120, 124, 136
larvae 5
leaders 17
leafhoppers 15
Leptoconops 28
Leptophlebia 25
letort hopper (fly illus.) 21
Libellula 32
light cahill (fly illus.) 20
lightning 103
Limnephilus 27
Little Bighorn River 38,144

Little Popo Agie River 38, 79, 123
Little Sandy Creek 97, 124
Little Wind River 79, 123, 149
Los Pinos River 70, 122, 137
mackinaw 3
Madison River 147, 148
malenka 29
Mancos River 70, 122
maps 40, 41
mayflies 11, 12
mayfly 5, 22-26
mayfly nymph (fly illus.) 18
measuring trout 34
Medicine Bow River 90, 124
Medicine Lodge Creek 38
Michigan River 136
Middle Fork of Powder River 38, 86, 123
Middle Fork of the South Platte River 37
Middle Popo Agie River 38
midge (fly illus.) 21
midge larva (fly illus.) 18
midges 8, 31
mollusks 5
Montana nymph (fly illus.) 19
mosquitoes 35
muddler minnow (fly illus.) 21
Nemoura 29-31
Neoperla 31
New Fork River 38, 94, 124
Niobara River 143
North Fork of Michigan River 45, 120
North Fork of Powder River 86, 123
North Fork of South Platte River 47, 120
North Fork of White River 66, 122
North Fork Powder River 38, 144
North Fork Shoshone River 38, 143
North French Creek 38

North Platte River 37, 38, 44, 88, 89, 120, 124, 136, 145
North Popo Agie River 38, 78, 123
North St. Vrain Creek 37, 48, 120
North Tongue River 38, 144
Nowood River 80, 123
nymphs 5
Oligophlebodes 27
organizations 128
Osier Creek 37, 137
otter shrimp (fly illus.) 21
Paint Rock Creek 39
parachute mayfly (fly illus.) 20
Paraleptophlebia 25
peak flow 42
photoperiods 6
Piedra River 68, 122, 137
Piney Creek 38
Plathemis 32
Platyphylax 27
pollution 6
Popo Agie River 143, 149
Poudre River (*see Cache la Poudre River*)
premium fishing 36
private property 35
Pseudocloeon 25, 26
Pteronarcella 31
Pteronarcys 31
quill gordon (fly illus.) 20
rainbow trout 3, 4, 5
Raphidia 28
rattlesnakes 34
red ant 15, 32
red quill (fly illus.) 20
Rhacophilia 28
Rhithrogena 26
Rio Grande 36, 72, 121, 136, 137
Rio Grande cutthroat 2
river basins 40, 41
Roaring Fork River 36, 37, 58, 121, 134, 135
Rock River 38

Rocky Mountain danger 34
Rocky Mountain National Park 139
Rocky Mountain tick spotted fever 34
royal coachman (fly illus.) 20
royal wulff (fly illus.) 20
Salmo aguabonita 2
Salmo clarki 2
Salmo clarkii henshawi 2
Salmo clarkii lewisi 2
Salmo clarkii pleuriticus 2
Salmo clarkii utah 2
Salmo clarkii virginalis 2
Salmo gairdneri 3
Salmo stomias 2
Salmo trutta 2
salmonfly 8, 31
Salt River 38, 101, 125, 141, 142
Salvelinus fontinalus 3
Salvelinus namaycush 3
San Francisco Creek 137
San Juan River 67, 68, 122, 137
Sand Creek 38, 143, 144
scud 15, 32
scud (fly illus.) 21
sculpin 5
sedge (fly illus.) 19
sedge 7
Sericostomitidae 28
Shell Creek 81, 123, 143
Shoshone River 38, 83, 123, 142, 143
shrimp 5, 15, 32
Sialis 32
Siphlonurus 26
Smith Fork River 38
Snake River 38, 98, 99, 125, 141, 142
Snake River cutthroat 2
snowmelt 42
Somatochlora 28
South Fork of White River 66, 122
South Fork Shoshone R 84, 123

South French Creek   39
South Piney Creek   39, 144
South Platte River   36, 37, 46,
   120, 137, 138, 145
South Tongue River   39, 144
spawning seasons   4
spinner fall   12
spinners   10, 12
St. Vrain Creek   138
standard deviation values
   120-125
standard deviations explanation
   43
Stenonema   26
stonefly   5, 8, 9, 29-31
stonefly nymph (fly illus.)   18
stores   127, 128
streamflow   42, 120-125
subimagos   11
Sunlight Creek   39
Sweetwater River   90, 91, 124,
   145
Sympetrum   32
synchronous hatching   11
Syphlonurus   12
Tarryall Creek   37, 47, 120
Taylor River   60, 121, 135, 136
temperature range   4
terrestrial insects   5, 6, 15
Thorofare Creek   39
thunderstorms   103
ticks   34, 35
Timber Creek   38
tippet   17
Tongue River   38, 39, 84, 85,
   123, 143, 144
Trappers Lake   37
Tricorythodes   12, 26
trout coloring   2, 3, 32, 33
trout diet   6
trout facts   2, 3
trout flies   18-21
trout parts   5
trout range   2, 3
trout stream beetle   15, 32

trout streams   42, 43
Trout Unlimited   128
U.S.G.S.   43
Uncompahgre River   63, 122
Utah cutthroat   2
Visoka   31
water temperature   4, 6, 42
weather conditions   102-119
weather rules of thumb   102
White River   67, 122, 134
Wild Trout Water   36
Williams Fork River   55, 64,
   121, 122
Willow Creek   54, 121
willow flies   8
wind chill   105
Wind River   38, 39, 77, 123,
   142, 143, 149
Wind River Indian Reservation
   149
worms   5
Wyoming Fishing Regulations
   140-149
Wyoming Fishing Zones Map
   141
Wyoming map   40
Wyoming Mileage Chart   129
Wyoming trout streams   74-101,
   122-125
Wyoming weather   114-119
Yampa River   65, 122, 134
Yellowstone cutthroat   2
Yellowstone fishing zones map
   146
Yellowstone River   39, 74, 75,
   122, 142, 143, 147, 148
Yellowstone National Park   147,
   148
zug bug (fly illus.)   18